**CAMBRIDGE
EXAMINATIONS
PUBLISHING**

CAE
Reading Skills

Simon Greenall
Diana Pye

CAMBRIDGE
UNIVERSITY PRESS

Published by the Press Syndicate of the University of Cambridge
The Pitt Building, Trumpington Street, Cambridge CB2 1RP
40 West 20th Street, New York, NY 10011–4211, USA
10 Stamford Road, Oakleigh, Melbourne 3166, Australia

© Cambridge University Press 1996

First published 1996

Printed in Great Britain at the University Press, Cambridge

A catalogue record for this book is available from the British Library

ISBN 0 521 45557 X

Contents

Map of the book

Unit	Title	Topics	Exam question types	Reading strategies
1	Foundation unit	The CAE exam	Multiple matching	All the strategies tested in the exam (see *To the teacher*)
2	Survival	Cold water survival Culture shock	Multiple matching: headings with sections of the text	Understanding main ideas, retrieving specific information, understanding the text as a whole, identifying information to perform a task, understanding writer's intention, inferring, dealing with difficult vocabulary
3	Consumer issues	How hidden persuasion makes shoppers spend Choosing burgers	Multiple matching: summary sentences with sections of text	Predicting, forming an overall impression, skimming for main ideas, retrieving specific information, dealing with difficult vocabulary, identifying information to perform a task
4	Transport	Aircraft Cycling in town	Multiple matching: headings with paragraphs	Predicting, forming an overall impression, understanding text organisation, skimming for main ideas, dealing with difficult vocabulary, inferring
5	Travel	Travel brochure on China Reviews of travel guides	Multiple matching: items of detail with places	Forming an overall impression, retrieving specific information, reading for specific information, identifying information to perform a task, inferring, dealing with difficult vocabulary
6	Large-scale art	The story of Christo, the sculptor An artist who uses large areas of land for artistic expression	Gapped text: inserting sentences which belong to a text	Forming an overall impression, understanding main ideas, identifying clues to text structure, retrieving specific information
7	Children and education	Teenagers in love with money The best way to teach a genius	Multiple matching: opinions with people	Interpreting opinions, predicting, inferring, forming an overall impression, retrieving specific information, evaluating the text
8	The oceans	Changes in the climate The route of shipwrecked trainers	Multiple-choice questions	Predicting, retrieving specific information dealing with difficult vocabulary, understanding text organisation, understanding main ideas, evaluating the text

Unit	Title	Topics	Exam question types	Reading strategies
9	Memorable incidents	A dangerous encounter with a shark A theft during a journey	Gapped text: inserting paragraphs which belong to a text	Forming an overall impression, understanding main ideas, retrieving specific information, understanding text organisation, interpreting purpose of sentences, dealing with difficult vocabulary
10	Cultural issues	Minority languages Cultural differences among nations	Multiple matching: figures to languages; completing sentences with phrases	Understanding main ideas, evaluating the text, inferring, retrieving specific information
11	The living world	The continued presence of wolves in Europe Animal intelligence	Multiple matching: completing sentences with phrases	Predicting, understanding main ideas, retrieving specific information, inferring, understanding writer's attitude and purpose, distinguishing between fact and opinion
12	Communications	The effect of fax machines Etiquette on the Internet	Multiple-choice questions	Inferring, understanding writer's attitude and tone, understanding writer's style, understanding main ideas, understanding writer's intention, understanding text organisation, dealing with difficult vocabulary
13	Science fiction?	Domestic help in the future Genetically engineered food	Gapped text: inserting paragraphs which belong to a text	Forming an overall impression, evaluating the text, understanding main ideas, understanding text organisation, predicting, inferring, retrieving specific information, interpreting writer's opinion, understanding writer's style
14	Modern life	Living longer today A critical look at psychoanalysis	Multiple-choice questions	Understanding main ideas, retrieving specific information, inferring, understanding writer's style, predicting
15	Other people, other ways	Smoking in the USA A traditional tribe in Pakistan	Gapped text: inserting sentences which belong to a text	Predicting, understanding main ideas, evaluating the text, identifying arguments for and against, understanding the writer's attitude, understanding text organisation, inferring, forming an overall impression
16	The world of work	Office life of the future How much work is done in meetings?	Multiple-choice questions	Predicting, understanding main ideas, retrieving specific information, inferring, understanding writer's opinion, dealing with difficult vocabulary

Thanks

We would like to thank:

Our editor Alison Silver, for her endless support, advice and care over this book.

Lindsay White, Jeanne McCarten, Liz Sharman, Joanne Currie, Peter Ducker and everybody at Cambridge University Press for making this book possible.

The authors and publishers would like to thank the following teachers and their students for piloting *CAE Reading Skills*:

John Ejsmond (British Institute, Florence)
Diane Fleming, Rosemary Hancock and Mike O'Neill (Institut Britànic, Barcelona)
Michael Jenkins (IALS, Edinburgh)
Pierrick Picot (Institut de Perfectionnement en Langues Vivantes, Angers)
Paul Power

Their detailed comments and constructive suggestions have helped us enormously.

To the student

About the exam

The Certificate in Advanced English (CAE) is for students at an advanced level of English. To give you an idea of the level, you may have taken the Cambridge First Certificate of English (FCE) and obtained a grade C or above. However, this is not essential if you want to sit the CAE.

There are five papers in the exam: Reading (Paper 1), Writing (Paper 2), English in Use (Paper 3), Listening (Paper 4), and Speaking (Paper 5). This book helps you prepare for Reading (Paper 1). You may like to use *CAE Writing Skills* and *CAE Listening and Speaking Skills* to help you prepare for Papers 2, 4 and 5.

Paper 1 (Reading) takes 1 hour 15 minutes to do, and contains four passages taken from newspapers, magazines and other sources. There are a number of different question types such as blank-filling, multiple-choice questions and matching exercises. You are usually required to choose an answer from a number of different options. It's a good idea to choose your answers carefully and write them on the exam paper, then transfer your answers in pencil to the Answer sheet. You can see an example of the Answer sheet on page 137 of this book, and it's a good idea to study it carefully before the exam so it will not come as a surprise when you take the exam.

The questions test a number of different reading skills, such as reading for main ideas, reading for specific information, understanding text organisation, inferring, dealing with unfamiliar words, and evaluating the text. These are all skills which you may already have acquired and developed in your language lessons so far, but which you need to be confident of using in the exam.

In your preparation for the exam, you should try to develop your skill in reading quickly, and as long as you give yourself plenty of practice in this, you will have more time for checking your answers in the exam.

About this book

This book is designed to give you practice in developing the different reading skills which are tested in the exam, and in answering the exam questions themselves. You need to be very familiar with the exam question types in order to answer them effectively.

You can use this book in class, alone or with a partner, or as self-study material working at home. The answers are at the back of the book, but try not to look at them before you've tried to answer the questions on your own.

There is a progression of difficulty, but you can dip into different units in any order you like. There are two sections in each unit, each taking about 60 minutes to do. Section A is concerned with exam-type questions, and Section

B focuses on the general reading skills you need to take the exam. In each section there are exam tips and study tips to help you. Unit 1 provides you with a great deal of information about the exam, which we hope you'll find useful.

We have chosen texts which we hope you will enjoy reading. Your motivation is extremely important in your preparation for the exam, and we have tried to provide texts and tasks which interest you.

Good luck with *CAE Reading Skills*, and good luck with the exam!

Diana Pye   **Simon Greenall**

To the teacher

Aims

CAE Reading Skills aims to help you prepare your candidates for Paper 1 (Reading) of the Certificate in Advanced English (CAE). Our principal aim is to provide systematic coverage of the specific skills needed for the Reading paper of the exam. However, in keeping with the declared spirit of the exam, which is designed to reflect current developments in methodology and teaching practice, as well as to test the candidates' language competence, our secondary aim is to provide a thorough presentation and development of the various skills needed for effective reading comprehension at an advanced level.

The book contains a great deal of information about the exam itself, and in particular, about the exam question types, about the strategies required to answer the questions successfully, and about the texts used.

You can use it as a self-study book, either in the classroom or for the candidate working at home. It can also be used interactively in the classroom if you require extra material to supplement the main course of preparation for the exam. While we give no explicit pairwork instructions, you can use most activities for discussion work. Although we have chosen text types which reflect those you would expect to find in the exam, we have also selected them with the interests and motivation of the non-examination class in mind. Even if you find yourself with a class in which some students have not yet decided to take the exam, you will be able to use the book for advanced level reading skills.

Organisation

The book is divided into sixteen units.

The Foundation unit (Unit 1) uses a 'loop' format in which information about the exam is presented using activities similar to the question types in the exam. Helping the candidates become familiar with the exam format is an important part of exam preparation, and we hope that you will find this approach useful and challenging.

The remaining fifteen units each focus on a specific exam question type, and are divided into two sections which are thematically linked. There is a balance between *exam-specific* and *exam-oriented* question types. *Exam-specific* question types are those used in the CAE exam which consist of various types of cloze (blank-filling) passages, multiple-choice questions (one stem in the form of a question or an incomplete statement, followed by four possible answers) and multiple-matching exercises (several stems usually in the form of incomplete statements with several possible answers). These items provide an objective test in so far as they always have a 'right answer'.

Here the emphasis is on accuracy rather than fluency and priority is given to the development and practice of the discrete skills tested in the exam. *Exam-oriented* question types are those which help develop the learner's mastery of reading skills and therefore his or her reading efficiency. These activities may be subjective and have no 'right answer'. They are designed to develop fluency. In general terms, Section A of each unit focuses on *exam-specific question types*, and Section B on *exam-oriented question types*, although you will find examples of both question types in both sections.

In Section A of each unit you will find:
– one or more exam-type texts
– a series of activities to contextualise the texts and activities and to prepare the candidates for reading
– an activity (or two) which prepares the candidates specifically for a particular exam question type
– a specific exam question
– an exam tip box, containing advice specific to the question type under scrutiny in the section
– follow-up activities and discussion work

In Section B of each unit you will find:
– one or more exam-type texts, linked thematically to those in the preceding section
– a series of activities contextualising the passage(s), developing the candidates' reading strategies in a way that is relevant to their level
– a study tip box, containing advice on how to develop their reading strategies
– follow-up activities and discussion work

Each section will take about 60 minutes to teach but you may find that the topics selected and material provided are rich enough to extend discussion beyond this time if the candidates' interest is sustained.

Texts

The texts are authentic and have been drawn from a wide range of sources, including newspapers, general interest magazines, leaflets, guides, etc., in order to familiarise students with the different text types and forms which they are expected to process in the CAE exam. Literary texts are not included since they do not form part of the exam.

We chose the texts for their interest value and the motivation they would generate in the classroom. In the exam, it might be claimed that the intrinsic interest of the text for the candidates is not so important, since the desire to pass the exam provides the principal source of motivation. Furthermore, in the exam the text chosen must meet other stringent criteria, most important of which is its potential to provide suitably rich material to base the test on. But in the classroom or in self-study use, there is both greater freedom and greater necessity to choose texts which will generate and sustain the candidates' motivation.

In the exam, the candidates are asked to read four lengthy texts in a comparatively short amount of time. Trials have shown that they are capable of doing this successfully when they have reached the standard required by the exam. We have made suggestions concerning the time limit to complete a task in order to build up the candidates' ability in speed reading.

Some of the criteria for creating and sustaining the candidates' motivation to read are:
– the relevance of the content and topic; the candidates are not motivated by issues that are of little or no concern to them
– an international and cross-cultural appeal; these aspects can usually be sure of creating genuine interest to read
– the provision of new information; it seems pointless to make the candidates read about something which they are already aware of, just because it happens to be in English

Not all of the criteria will be met in every text, and some of the criteria overlap. However, some or all of these criteria must be met if the material is to be used successfully in the class or for self-study.

Question types

In the book, priority is given to the development and practice of the discrete skills tested in the exam. These are:
– to form an overall impression by skimming the text
– to retrieve specific information by scanning the text
– to interpret texts for inference, attitude and style
– to demonstrate understanding of the text as a whole
– to select relevant information required to perform a task
– to demonstrate understanding of how text structure operates
– to deduce meaning from context

The questions, tasks and activities in the book are all designed to deconstruct the exam question by analysing the stages in reading comprehension which the candidate needs to pass through in order to answer it successfully.

An interesting feature of many of the question types in the exam is that they are innovatory not only for an exam but also for classroom use. They can therefore contribute as much as the texts themselves towards motivating the candidates.

There are two kinds of *exam-oriented* tasks: principal and secondary tasks. Principal tasks are designed to lead the candidates to the heart of the text, to the reason why it was written. This means that there will be at least one task which encourages the candidate to read the text for its main ideas, and others which focus on pre-reading and prediction work. If the vocabulary of the text is likely to get in the way of effective comprehension, then there may also be a question which helps the candidates deal with unfamiliar words.

Secondary tasks focus on less important, although no less interesting aspects of the text, and explore further the topic and the issues raised.

Suggestions for use

It was mentioned earlier that the book can be used for self-study or interactively in the classroom. As self-study material, it can be used for home study or in the classroom. Encourage your candidates to choose the units which interest them, or direct them to units which provide practice in areas in which you consider they could benefit from some improvement. During a later lesson, it is a good idea to find out how successfully they have worked alone by checking if they have answered the questions correctly.

As interactive classroom material, you may also want to leave out certain units and exercises, or spend more time on some parts than on other parts. You can let students work alone or in pairs. All the activities can be used for discussion practice even though this is not specified in the instructions.

There is a progression in the difficulty of the book so you can use it as an extended course of systematic training for the exam. But it is also expected that you may want to dip into it in a random way, using it as a resource to supplement your existing main course of training. Both approaches are equally appropriate.

The exam tips are often placed before the exam question they refer to and students will read the tips before they answer the question. On some occasions you may want to let them do the activity and then read the advice. They can then do the activity again, with the advice in mind, to see if they are more successful. The position of the study tips is similar.

When you come to an exam tip or a study tip, here are some suggestions on classroom procedure:
- ask the students to read the information to themselves
- ask them to summarise the information from memory with a partner
- find out if anyone believes they already use the strategies suggested, or were aware of the information given in the box
- find out if they can remember what the preceding exam tip or study tip contained, and if the advice is relevant to anything they have done in the present section
- ask them to do, or redo, the question which the advice refers to
- ask them to decide if the information is useful

There is a deliberate attempt to recycle and revise the tips in a systematic way.

The book was written with pleasure, and is intended to be used with pleasure, with special emphasis on the flexibility of use. We hope you enjoy using *CAE Reading Skills*.

Diana Pye   **Simon Greenall**

1

Foundation unit

When you read outside the classroom context you usually know where the text comes from or who it was written for. When you read something in class or in an exam this may not be the case and the first thing you need to do is to *skim* the text to form an overall impression about the type of text, the topic, etc. Try not to worry about any difficult words because you are not focusing on details of the text at this stage.

1 ⌨ Look quickly at the text on page 8 and decide where it comes from. Try to do this activity in no more than 30 seconds. Choose from the following:

a) a newspaper
b) an examination specifications leaflet

c) an advertisement
d) an examination paper

What helped you make up your mind?

Whether you read in your own language or in a foreign language, it is important to try to understand the meaning of the text as a whole, to extract the main ideas. This is also a skimming activity but may require more time and a more careful reading. It's useful to look at the title of the text and paragraph headings to decide what is the important information and what isn't. Once again, try to ignore any words you don't understand.

2 ⌨ Match the headings 1–9 below with the paragraphs of the text. Two headings are already given and there are two extra headings. Try to take no more than two minutes.

1 Paper 1 Reading *(1¼ hours)*
2 Paper 5 Speaking *(15 minutes)*
3 Reading strategies
4 Paper 3 English in Use *(1 hour 30 minutes)*

5 Certification
6 Exam tasks
7 Level
8 Intended population
9 Paper 4 Listening *(45 minutes)*

What helped you make up your mind?

A | Introduction

The Certificate in Advanced English (CAE) is an examination in reading, writing, the structure of the language, listening and speaking, at post-First Certificate level. Launched in December 1991, it is offered twice yearly in June and December.

B |

The examination offers a high-level final qualification in the language to those wishing to use English for professional or study purposes. CAE is also designed to encourage the development of the skills required by students progressing towards the Cambridge Proficiency examination (CPE), with the emphasis very much on real-world tasks.

C |

The population for the examination ranges from adolescents to young professional people. The examination consists of five papers which are outlined below. There are no set texts and no optional papers. All papers receive equal weighting (i.e. 20%).

D |

Contains four texts selected to test a wide range of reading skills and strategies with various types of matching and multiple-choice items.

E | Paper 2 Writing *(2 hours)*

Consists of two compulsory tasks of approximately 250 words each. No choice is offered for the first task. The second task is selected from a choice of four. All tasks are contextualised; purpose and intended audience are specified.

F |

The three sections of this paper test the ability to apply knowledge of the language system, including control of grammar, register, cohesion, spelling and punctuation.

G |

Contains four texts of varying length and nature selected to test a wide range of listening skills with various types of matching, completion and multiple-choice items.

H |

Candidates are examined in pairs by two external examiners. The four phases of the paper are designed to elicit a wide range of speaking skills and strategies from both candidates.

I |

Certificates for successful candidates carry an overall grade: A, B or C. Certificates are not issued to candidates awarded the failing grades, D, E and U. Result slips for candidates who fail provide an indication of those papers in which their performance is particularly weak. Result slips for candidates who pass provide an indication of those papers in which an outstanding performance has been achieved.

When you read something to select information in order to perform a particular task you don't normally read the whole text in detail, you probably only read the information which is relevant to your purposes. For example, when you look in a travel guide for interesting places to visit, you are unlikely to read the whole guide; when you buy electrical equipment you probably read the instructions leaflet before using it. Can you think of other examples?

3 ⌀ This activity requires you to select information about the sort of people who the CAE exam is suitable for.

Read these descriptions of four students of English. Who would you recommend the CAE exam to? Who would you discourage from taking it? Can you say why?

Louise is 20 and has just finished a hotel management course. She has decided to take the Cambridge First Certificate exam next year but in the meantime she thinks she needs more basic practice.

Julia is 18 and has just left school. She has not yet made up her mind exactly what she would like to do so she has decided to spend six months improving her English. She studied English at school for seven years.

Sato works for a British firm in Osaka. He is ambitious and hopes to be promoted and given the opportunity to travel. He studied English literature at university but finds it difficult to communicate on a day-to-day basis.

Reza has the opportunity of a job with an airline company in the Middle East. He has the necessary professional qualifications but no certificate to attest to his level of English. He has enrolled on a Cambridge Proficiency course but is worried he may not pass the exam.

A similar process is when you scan the text to retrieve specific information. Often it is a matter of spotting the words which are relevant to your particular purpose.

4 This activity demonstrates the strategy of scanning.

Look at the exam specifications again. Write down the words and expressions which show why CAE is a suitable exam for you.

Texts are structured by a series of ideas in a logical order. The order may be indicated by any of the following:

- typographical conventions (such as *italics*, CAPITALS, **bold type**)
- punctuation and abbreviations (such as commas, dashes, *e.g., i.e., etc.*)
- pronoun reference (such as *he, she, who, which*)
- clause structure (words like *than* and *in order to* require certain types of clause to precede them)
- discourse markers (such as *and, but, although, however, including*)
- the subject matter itself
- or more usually, by a combination of some or all of these

5 ⌁ These four sentence endings are taken from *Recommendations for Candidate Preparation* for the Reading paper of the CAE exam. Decide where they should go in the text below. There are six suggested places, but only four are correct.

1 – deduce meaning from context.
2 ..., including the 'science/technology for the lay person' texts featured in newspapers and magazines.
3 ... rather than to concentrate on the meaning of every word in the text.
4 ... which aims to test a candidate's ability to cope with authentic texts.

RECOMMENDATIONS FOR CANDIDATE PREPARATION

The CAE Reading paper is designed to test a range of reading skills:

- form an overall impression by skimming the text;
- retrieve specific information by scanning the text;
- interpret text for inference, attitude and style;
- demonstrate understanding of text as a whole;
- select relevant information required to perform a task;
- demonstrate understanding of how text structure operates;

....

These skills reflect the real-world needs of large numbers of learners/users of English at an advanced level, i.e. the processing of large amounts of text, of different types and in a variety of format, in real time .... The CAE Reading paper therefore places emphasis on reading strategies.

Candidates need training in developing reading strategies and skills for successful completion of the Reading paper. Candidates should be exposed during the preparation phase to a wide range of text types and sources .... Training is needed in processing texts, and in information-transfer techniques and tasks. Candidates should be encouraged to extract from a text the information required to perform a given task .... CAE candidates also need to develop the skill of deducing meaning from the context, ... making use of predictive strategies as well as of the clues in a text. Candidates should not expect the texts on the Reading paper to include only words they are familiar with; this would be unrealistic, and undesirable in an examination ....

Centres should ensure that candidates for the CAE Reading paper are familiar with the technique of indicating their answers on the separate answer sheet and that they are trained to do this quickly and accurately.

(Adapted by permission of the University of Cambridge Local Examinations Syndicate)

TIP

Sometimes a writer doesn't say something explicitly but the reader may be able to read between the lines to infer what the writer means.

6 Try this activity, which asks you to interpret the text for inference.

The text on page 10 lays down guidelines for the preparation of candidates for the CAE exam. However, it does not explicitly say what the exam consists of. What can you infer about the exam paper from the information in the text? Think about:

- length of texts
- text types
- vocabulary content
- amount of time
- tasks set in the exam
- answer sheet

7 The Reading paper of the CAE exam is marked by computer, and you will therefore be required to transfer your answers to an optically marked (OMR) answer sheet.

Look carefully at the specimen OMR sheet on page 137 and decide whether these statements and instructions are true or false. If they are false can you correct them?

1 Write your name and the name of the invigilator in the spaces provided.
2 Only use a pencil on the answer sheet.
3 Only sign your OMR sheet when you have checked the information on it.
4 Some questions may have more than one answer.
5 If you make a mistake you can either use an eraser or correcting fluid.
6 You show your answer by writing a number and a letter.
7 Shade in the answer lozenge taking care not to make any other marks on the paper.
8 For questions which require a full, written answer you should use the spaces provided at the bottom of the OMR sheet.

8 Write down as much information about the Reading paper of the CAE exam as you can remember.

Look back at the texts in this unit and check.

Survival

The aim of this unit is to focus on the following:

– understanding a text as a whole and identifying the aim of a text

– skimming a text for the main ideas without reading in detail

The multiple-matching exam question requires you to match headings with sections of the text.

Section A

1 ☛ Look quickly at the text opposite and decide which of the following you are likely to find it in:

a) a newspaper   d) a science magazine
b) a tourist brochure   e) a text book
c) a safety leaflet   f) a guide book

2 ☛ Which of the following does the text aim to do?

a) present research results on hypothermia
b) warn people of the dangers of boating
c) instruct people on what they should do if they fall into cold water
d) describe a boating accident

Who do you think it is designed for?

EXAM TIP

For each question on the Reading paper you will be told what type of text you are dealing with – a holiday brochure, a newspaper or magazine article, or, as in the exam question in this section, a leaflet – and the topic of the text. If you know what type of text you are going to read and what the text is about, you are likely to find it easier to identify the aim of the text.

The aim of the leaflet in this section is to instruct and advise people. You would therefore expect this type of text to be fairly straightforward and to state information clearly.

The exam question on page 15 asks you to match headings with sections of the leaflet. The main difficulty of this task is the large amount of text you have to deal with in a short time. Because the aim of the question is to test your ability to identify the main ideas of the text, try not to waste time reading the whole text in detail, but skim through it in order to identify the main ideas.

COLD WATER
SURVIVAL

A

Hypothermia is the lowering of deep body temperature that places the body in a general state of shock, which in turn depresses normal body functions.

In cold water, the skin cools very rapidly. However, it takes 10–15 minutes before the temperature of the heart, brain and other internal organs begins to drop. Intense shivering occurs in an attempt to increase the body's heat production and counteract the large heat loss. Once cooling begins, the body temperature falls steadily and unconsciousness can occur. Cardiac arrest is the usual cause of death when the temperature cools to below 30°C.

B | How long can one survive in cold water?

The experimental average predicted survival times of average men and women holding still in ocean water and wearing a standard lifejacket and light clothing is about 2½–3 hours in water of 10°C (50°F). Predicted survival time is increased by extra body fat and decreased by small body size. Although women generally possess slightly more fat than men they cool slightly faster due to their usually small body size.

Children are particularly vulnerable to cold water, because they are smaller and have less fat than adults. In the event of a family being immersed, it is important for the parents to either get children partially or completely out of the water or on some form of flotation (e.g. an overturned boat). A little boy should be pulled out of the water first because he loses heat faster than his twin sister. If no flotation is available the adults should sandwich the child between them to help equalise the cooling rates of all involved.

Flotation lifejackets provide significant thermal protection and increase predicted survival time by more than 75%.

C

No! Although the body produces almost three times as much heat when swimming slowly and steadily in cold water compared to holding still, this extra heat is lost to the cold water due to more blood circulation to the arms, legs and skin. Results show that the person swimming in a lifejacket cools 35% faster than when holding still.

D

On occasion, the shore may be close enough to reach despite a faster cooling rate with this activity. Tests conducted on people swimming in ocean water of 10°C (50°F) and wearing standard lifejackets and light clothing showed that the average person could cover only a short distance before being incapacitated by hypothermia. This distance will obviously be affected by one's swimming ability, amount of insulation and water conditions. It is not easy to judge distance and the shore may appear to be closer than it actually is.

In cold water, an individual is likely to be able to swim a distance of no more than ⅒th of what he or she could easily swim in warm water.

In most instances, the best advice is to stay with the boat!

E

In this unfortunate situation, one is forced to adopt the "anti-drowning" technique of treading water.

Treading water involves continuous movement of the arms and legs in various patterns in order to keep the head out of the water. Test results show an average cooling rate of persons treading water that was 34% faster than while holding still in a lifejacket.

F | What body regions lose heat quickly?

The head and neck are the most critical heat loss areas. Infra-red pictures show that the sides of the chest and the groin are also major routes for heat loss. If an effort is made to conserve body heat, these regions deserve special attention.

G

Based on the heat loss information in section F, two techniques were tested that attempted to reduce heat loss from critical areas.

HELP (Heat Escape Lessening Position)

This technique involves holding the inner side of the arms tight against the side of the chest. The thighs are pressed together. This body position was indeed a significant help, resulting in nearly a 50% increase in predicted survival time.

Huddle

"Common sense" would predict longer survival time with huddling. Studies show that if the huddle is formed so that the sides of the chest of different persons are held close together, a 50% increase in predicted survival time is obtained.

H	**Does it help to get your body out of the water?**

The answer is almost invariably yes. The body surrenders its heat to the water many times more quickly than to air of the same temperature.

Therefore, if possible, get on top of an overturned boat or any wreckage that is available.

I	

Contrary to popular belief, alcoholic beverages do not warm a person and under no circumstances should they be given to a hypothermic casualty. Alcohol dilates the blood vessels and may increase heat loss. It also interferes with one's ability to think clearly.

J	

All hypothermic casualties should be handled gently, avoiding jolts that might adversely affect the heart's function.

- Get them out of the water to a dry, sheltered area.
- DO NOT RUB THE SURFACE OF THE BODY.
- Remove wet clothing – if possible put on layers of dry clothing – cover the head and neck (hat/scarf).
- Apply warm (40–45°C) objects such as wet towels, water bottles, chemical heat packs (hand warmers) to head, neck and trunk. BE CAREFUL TO AVOID BURNS.
- Give warm drinks for mild hypothermic cases only – NEVER ALCOHOL, COFFEE, TEA OR COCOA.
- In severe cases donate heat to the trunk of the body by direct body contact, especially to the chest, with warm person(s). The rescuer should remove upper clothing and huddle with the casualty inside blankets/sleeping bags.

3 🔁 **Look quickly through the text and decide which sections are about the points below. Some of the sections may be used more than once, while others may not be used at all. Try and take no more than five minutes.**

1 children's survival time ....

2 how a lifejacket influences heat loss ....

3 the importance of shivering ....

4 how movement influences body heat loss ....

5 how body position can influence survival time ....

6 what to do with someone who has been immersed in cold water

....

7 how body size influences heat loss ....

8 the cause of death ....

4 🔊 *Exam Question* For questions **1–7**, choose the most suitable heading for the various sections of the safety leaflet from list **A–J** below. Three headings are given as examples in the text.

1	Section A	**A**	How far can I swim?
2	Section C	**B**	What if I have no lifejacket or flotation?
3	Section D	**C**	What behaviour will increase survival time?
4	Section E	**D**	What about children?
5	Section G	**E**	Does alcohol consumption affect survival time?
6	Section I	**F**	How do you warm someone who has been in cold water?
7	Section J	**G**	Do different types of lifejackets offer more or less thermal protection?
		H	What is hypothermia and how does it kill?
		I	Should I swim to keep warm?
		J	Do people ever die of shock when falling into cold water?

5 🔊 **Decide if the following statements are true or false. Correct them where necessary.**

1 Children lose heat more slowly than adults.
2 Shivering is a useful way of counteracting heat loss.
3 Women are more resistant than men because of their size.
4 Swimming slowly helps you keep warm and therefore reduces overall heat loss.
5 Alcohol should only be given to people suffering from mild hypothermia.
6 Survival chances are better if you can get out of the water.
7 Children can survive for longer than adults because they are smaller.
8 Shock is the most frequent cause of death in cold water.
9 The head and neck should be kept warm whenever possible.
10 A person can only swim short distances in cold water.

6 🔊 **What should you do in the following circumstances to increase your chances of survival?**

1 You accidentally fall out of a boat without your companions seeing the accident. You have no lifejacket and the coast is out of sight.
2 Your boat overturns and you can't right it. You are alone with two children, a boy and a girl.
3 Three of you (two adults and a child) fall out of your small boat. You only have one lifejacket. The shore is within swimming distance for a competent swimmer.

7 **Have you ever been rescued from a dangerous situation?**

Section B

1 The passage in this section is about surviving culture shock when you're in a foreign country. Have you lived for a long time in a foreign country? How did you survive in the foreign culture? If you haven't, what problems do you think you might have?

Culture shock

My own experiment with culture shock came to an abortive end when I returned prematurely and gravely homesick from a year's study in Italy. I had never heard of culture shock. All I knew was that I was unhappy and wanted to go home.

That was twenty years ago, and since then culture shock has become a *bona fide* field of study. It is now understood that any normal person, finding him or herself for an extended time in a new culture, is in for trouble.

After all, our ideas on how to behave were formed in our early years. Nobody explained that we were learning standards applicable only in our own culture, that across the border things were done differently. We were taught that we were learning how to do things right. Consequently, when we turn up in a foreign land, the ways of others look simply wrong.

Left and right, people are behaving in ways you find unpredictable. Something seems terribly wrong, but you don't know what it is. Like me, you may just want to go home.

1

The process of "culture shock" is now recognized as so predictable that its four stages have been codified. The first is the honeymoon stage, familiar to those of us who love to travel, but never stay in one place long enough to find out what follows. In the honeymoon stage, the new country and its people seem delightful. Better than home. Everything is so different and charming, the people so nice, the customs so interesting.

2

Then the bloom comes off the rose. Now the people start to look shallow, selfish, stupid. The different ways of doing things don't seem interesting any more – just wearing. You start to feel tired all the time. Culture shock has set in. You feel at sea.

This response, stage two, could not be more natural. You are surrounded by people who grew up absorbing this culture, and you don't know how to do simple things. Even if you speak the language, you simply cannot understand the way people behave. You have lost a part of your identity, that self who back at home was confident and masterly.

2 The writer describes four stages of culture shock using these headings:

All at sea   The honeymoon   Acceptance   Adjusting

In what order do you expect to find them in the passage? What do you expect the writer to say about each stage?

STUDY TIP

The title, sub-titles and paragraph headings of a passage may give you clues to the content of the text, so it is a good idea to read them carefully and try to predict what the text is about. You may also need to recognise the type of text, who it was written for, and possibly something about the writer, because, in the classroom and in exams, reading passages are often presented out of context. All this information will help you understand the detailed meaning of a passage.

3 ⚏ Read the passage and match the headings in 2 with the numbers. Try to take no more than five minutes.

The emotional response to culture shock can be extreme. Confusion, depression, anxiety, and resentment can all enter to varying degrees. You may become physically ill. Little things seem terribly annoying. A perceived insult reduces you to tears.

At this point, many foreigners are tempted to retreat to an enclave of foreigners. They can be a great comfort, but also a danger.

If your fellow emigrés steadily reinforce your negative feelings about Americans, you may move into a sub-community of foreigners, and Americans will remain ever-strange to you. The shock may wear off, but you are still uncomfortable and homesick.

3 ⃞

The happier resolution is to move on to stage three. The old hands among your countrymen reassure you that they once felt as you do now. Rather than item-izing what's "wrong" with Americans, you remind yourself that "right" and "wrong" are not meaning-ful terms in cultural matters.

Instead, you try to understand what motivates Americans, perhaps realizing that many of the things you don't like are related to the things you do like (such as weak family ties and freedom; the fast pace and opportunity).

If you try to keep an open mind, take time to learn about America, and mix with Americans, your prog-nosis is good. It's important at this stage not to stay at home and mope but to get out and find things you like to do. And keep on studying the language.

4 ⃞

Within six months or a year of arrival – longer for some people – you should be moving into stage four, which is acceptance. At this point, you simply don't think any more about the peculiarities of Americans. You accept them as individuals.

You have started to feel at home; you know how to do things. You have not rejected your old culture; but the American ways have settled upon you. You feel optimistic about your future here. You should. You have truly arrived.

Esther Wanning

4 🔑 Who do you think the passage was written for?

   a) foreigners coming to the USA for a short visit
   b) foreigners coming to the USA for a long stay
   c) Americans going abroad for a short visit
   d) Americans going abroad for a long stay

What nationality is the writer?

5 🔑 Look at these sentences which are taken from the passage. Do they describe an *effect* of culture shock or *advice* on how to avoid it?

   1 'Something seems terribly wrong, but you don't know what it is.'
   2 'Everything is so different and charming, the people so nice, the customs so interesting.'
   3 'Little things seem terribly annoying.'
   4 '...you remind yourself that "right" and "wrong" are not meaningful terms in cultural matters.'
   5 'It's important at this stage not to stay at home and mope but to get out and find things you like to do.'

6 🔑 Answer the questions about these words or expressions:

   1 '...culture shock has become a *bona fide* field of study.' Does this mean it is now an acceptable or unacceptable field of study?
   2 'Then the bloom comes off the rose.' Does this mean that the foreign country appears as delightful as it did in the honeymoon stage or does it appear less delightful?
   3 'You feel at sea.' Is this likely to mean that you feel comfortable or confused?
   4 'The old hands among your countrymen...' Are these people who've been in America a long time or who have only just arrived?
   5 'It's important at this stage not to stay at home and mope...' Does *mope* mean something like *be depressed* or *be happy*?

7 🔑 Find evidence for these statements in the passage. Where there is no evidence, decide what the passage really says.

   1 Culture shock didn't use to be identified as a problem.
   2 There is a right and wrong way to do things.
   3 At first a foreign country may appear better than your own.
   4 After a while in a foreign culture you may lose confidence.
   5 Weak family ties and fast pace may appear as positive aspects, and freedom and opportunity may appear as negative aspects.
   6 Learning English will help you get over culture shock.
   7 The writer got over her culture shock very quickly.

8 Do you know any Americans? Which of the following words would you
use to describe them? Which words do you think they would like to use
to describe themselves?

> formal noisy friendly materialistic lazy greedy relaxed
> sincere sentimental slow hard-working

Think of words you can use to describe people from your country. Do
you think people from other countries would use the same words to
describe you?

9 What do you or would you do to avoid culture shock during a long stay
in a foreign country?

3

Consumer issues

The aim of this unit is to focus on the following:

- predicting what a text is about
- skimming for main ideas
- dealing with difficult vocabulary

The multiple-matching exam question requires you to match summary sentences with sections of the text.

Section A

1 Where do you generally do your food shopping?

- at a big out-of-town supermarket
- at a medium sized supermarket in the centre of town
- at the local grocer's
- at an outdoor market

Which of the following points do you consider important in your choice of shopping place?

convenience   service   prices   personal contacts
quality of products   variety of products   opening hours
speed of service   parking facilities   quality of environment
proximity of other services

2 ⚎ **The title of the newspaper article in this section is** *How hidden persuasion makes shoppers spend.* **Look quickly through the article and choose the description you think is closest to the likely content of the article:**

a) the increasing number of supermarkets
b) the popularity of out-of-town shopping centres
c) the tactics used to encourage customers to spend more money
d) the increased spending power of modern families

EXAM TIP

The multiple-matching exam question below tests your ability to recognise and understand the main ideas expressed in a text. You are asked to match sentences with marked sections of the text. The sentences briefly describe what the sections are about. The sections may consist of one or more paragraphs and not all the sections may be needed. When identifying the main ideas of a text it is not necessary to read in great detail, so try not to worry too much about difficult vocabulary, especially if it is not relevant to the task.

You may find this step-by-step approach useful:

– study titles, layout and graphics for clues to general meaning
– read quickly through the text underlining important words or sentences
– match the more obvious sentences without reading in detail
– read more carefully the sections where the answers are less obvious
– finally, if there are more sections than sentences, carefully check those you do not use

3 ⚎ *Exam Question*   For questions **1–8**, answer by choosing from the sections of the article **A–H** on page 22. Note: When more than one answer is required, these may be given in any order. Try to take no more than 15 minutes.

Which section talks about
how supermarket size influences sales?   **1** ☐
the advantages of Sunday trading?   **2** ☐
which brands are the most profitable?   **3** ☐ **4** ☐
how essential products are displayed and priced?   **5** ☐
how supermarket customers' shopping behaviour is
    studied?   **6** ☐
specific factors designed to increase sales?   **7** ☐
the way the interiors of supermarkets are designed?   **8** ☐

How hidden persuasion makes shoppers spend

Counter culture: James Erlichman looks at the subtle psychology gearing soft sell to big profits.

A

ENTERING a supermarket is like taking a seat in the psychiatrist's chair – the food shopper's deepest desires will be laid open and explored. In-store cameras backed up by discreet human surveillance measure when and where we are tempted to pause and drop that unnecessary little luxury into the trolley. The laser beam at the check-out records whether more mozzarella cheese is being sold after it was moved to an eye-catching display or featured in the supermarket's latest TV advertisement. Everything is geared to increased sales and profits, which means getting consumers to buy things they don't really need, but cannot resist.

B

Supermarkets don't like talking openly about tactics. They wish to appear the friendly grocer who helps wash our salads, not our brains. However, it is hard to disguise that virtually every new superstore has its primary doors on the left so the shopping is done clockwise, to the right. "Nine out of ten people are right handed and they prefer turning to the right," said Wendy Godfrey, a spokeswoman for Sainsbury's, one major supermarket chain.

C

Profits from the store's own label products are normally higher than those from the big manufacturers. So own label baked beans are usually placed to the left of the Heinz display because the eye reads left to right and will spot the store's brand first. The big manufacturers can rectify this by paying a premium for better display. How much they pay – especially when they may well be making the own brand version for the supermarket – is a closely guarded secret.

D

Of the 16,000 items of food which a superstore displays, only about 200 are KVIs – known value items – essentials such as tea, butter and coffee, the price of which will be known by most customers. Two rules apply here. Firstly, keep the cost competitive, which means halving gross profit margins to 15 per cent. Second, dot the KVIs around the store, so customers will have to hunt them out and walk past the frozen black forest gateau, or mangetout peas – items they do not really need.

E

Can a store be too big, threatening and confusing for the customer? Current thinking is that abundance sells. A well-stocked 20-foot display of tomato ketchup sells more sauce than a depleted shelf 15 feet long. "I don't think there is a maximum size unless it is how fast the average customer can get round without the frozen food defrosting," said John Davidson, a lecturer in retail marketing at the University of Surrey.

F

"Lighting influences the customer," he said. "It is kept soft in the wine section to encourage browsing, but it is sharp and bright at the cosmetics counter to suggest cleanliness." Width of aisles is also a factor. "If they move too fast they are missing buying opportunities," said Andy Mitchell, research officer with the Institute of Grocery Distribution. "They also try to bounce you back and forth across the aisle by putting the best-selling digestive biscuit on one side and the most popular chocolate one on the other."

G

Convenience and cost are also behind Sunday trading. Round-the-clock running of freezer and chill cabinets means supermarkets cost a lot to operate after closing. Many perishables thrown away on Saturday afternoon could be sold on Sunday. Just as important, however, is the psychology of leisure shopping. International studies show that people buy more expensive, discretionary items when they are relaxed and browsing.

H

It is not only how much one buys, but what one buys. A supermarket makes more profit from its own brand, microwave cooked-chill chicken kiev than it does from the ingredients needed to make it at home. Many consumers appear willing to pay almost any price to avoid preparing food. Grated carrots wrapped in a nice plastic bag sell briskly for £1.18 a pound at Sainsbury's. Whole carrots, a few feet away, cost just 19p a pound.

4 ┳○ Match the following headings with the various sections of the article.

1 Known Value Items   Section A ☐
2 Abundance Sells   Section B ☐
3 Sunday Trading   Section C ☐
4 Research Methods   Section D ☐
5 Product Specific Tactics Section E ☐
6 Own Label Products   Section F ☐
7 Store Layout   Section G ☐
8 Convenience Products Section H ☐

5 ┳○ A number of sales tactics are mentioned in the article.
Example: Main doors are on the left so that people move clockwise around the store.
Look at the article again and find six more sales tactics.

6 ┳○ Find the following sentences in the article and answer the questions about the words and expressions *in italics*. What is their meaning in the context?

1 'In-store cameras *backed up by* discreet human surveillance …' Does this mean that cameras are not the only means of watching people?
2 'Everything *is geared to* increased sales and profits, …' Are increased sales and profits a priority?
3 '… the eye reads left to right and will *spot* the store's brand first.' Why is the store's own label displayed to the left of other brands?
4 'Second, *dot* the KVIs *around* the store, …' Are the KVIs all likely to be grouped together?
5 '… so customers will have to *hunt them out* …' Are they likely to be easy or difficult to find?
6 'It is kept soft in the wine section to encourage *browsing*, …' Are shoppers likely to spend more or less time in the wine section?
7 'They also try to *bounce you back and forth across* the aisle …' Are things arranged so they are easy to find?

Use a dictionary to check.

7 Why do you think supermarkets do not like talking openly about sales tactics? Do you think that if you are aware of the various tactics used to encourage you to spend, these tactics are less likely to work?

Section B

1 Are you a hamburger enthusiast or do you avoid fast-food restaurants? Have you ever been to a McDonald's restaurant? Which of these words do you associate with McDonald's?

convenient	waste	American	ketchup	delicious
young	healthy	controversial	global	salad
balanced	culture	recycle	boring	horrible
expensive	tasty	aggressive	friendly	

2 Write a few sentences saying how you feel about fast food using words from the list.

3 🔑 Look quickly at the article and decide what type of text it is. Choose from the following:

a) a guide to the best fast-food restaurants
b) a report on a comparative test of different burgers
c) a report on the nutritional value of fast food
d) a number of recipes for burgers

4 Read the introductory section on pages 24 and 25 and underline all the words and expressions which are unfamiliar to you.

CHOICE BURGERS
Helen Lowry tries out the American way of beef on some young foodies

Anybody who paid $2,250 for 100 shares when McDonald's was floated in 1965 would have been a shrewd investor. The burger, reviled by environmentalists, revered by children, has become a cultural institution. But behind the façade of convenience and "have a nice day" lie ruthless marketing instincts and elaborate organisation. Global champ McDonald's is spreading into developing markets, where its image as an icon of Americana makes it hugely popular (one of its seven restaurants in Poland holds the world record for first-day sales, having served 33,000 customers).

In Britain its main competitor is Burger King which has recently made its way into 16 big British Rail stations – something of a coup considering more than £500 million is spent on fast food in Britain by rail or road travellers. Wimpy, the first American-style fast-food restaurant in Britain, is now mainly table service, as are Starburger, Julie's Pantry (based at motorway service areas) and Tootsies.

Nutritional content varies (Burger King, McDonald's and Wimpy all provide nutrition and ingredient information), but recipes, cooking methods and portion sizes are more or less standardised.

Most fast-food chains no longer use containers made with CFCs, so the focus of environmental concern has switched to the amount of packaging used. Many chains are responding with minor changes such as smaller bags and napkins. Most use some recycled packaging, but none recycle all their waste; McDonald's and Burger King have tried pilot recycling schemes and plan to extend them. Our testers, undeterred by any such concerns, are Ben Chespon, George Mayou, Louise Bakker and Alexander Scott-Tong, all aged 10.

Julie's Pantry (Prices range from £1.30 to £2.65)

The burgers were not top notch. There was too much meat and mayonnaise for George, and Alexander thought the uncooked slab of cheese in the hamburger "horrible". The bread was soft but there was far too much sauce with the Quarterpounder.

McDonald's (Prices range from 84p to £1.81)

Great expectations were on the whole fulfilled. Ben praised the crispy vegetables and mayonnaise. Alex liked the soft bread, chewy meat and mayonnaise but Louise couldn't deal with the Big Mac, describing it as "sick". She also felt it contained too many vegetables and didn't like the relish. George didn't like the mayonnaise but was delighted that the tomato ketchup ration was just right. There was praise also for the cheese. Overall the cheeseburger scored highest.

Burger King (Prices range from 84p to £1.78)

The Burger King Whopper was very popular, winning praise for the soft bread and chewy meat. Ben particularly enjoyed the crisp vegetables and gave this burger his top marks, though he thought the bread was rather rough and dry. Alex found the bread a bit chewy and thought the vegetables were too cold. Louse didn't like the hard pickles and agreed about the bread being dry. George found the amount of vegetables overwhelming.

Starburger (Prices range from 85p to £2.25)

The meat was described by the children as having a peanut butter taste, not unpleasant but a bit salty. George took out his vegetables, and Louise didn't like the salad, which contributed to the salt problem. It was agreed that the burgers without added ketchup were better. Ben liked the bread here but found the

meat greasy. The plain burger, it was thought, had too much tomato ketchup.

Wimpy (Prices range from 95p to £2.25)

George particularly liked the bacon burger, with its tasty cheese and crispy vegetables. Alex liked the "delicious soft bread". Overall he thought the burgers a bit better than McDonald's. George was so impressed that he asked the Wimpy people for information on how they cooked the meat ("not on a conveyor belt" was the answer).

7–11 (Prices range from £1.16 to £1.25)

Smaller than the rest, these burgers, according to the children, had too many onions and the bread was hard. The meat was praised as being nice and soft. The sesame bun was much appreciated, but there were no vegetables and the cheese portion seemed on the small side.

Tootsies (Regular quarterpounder £3.95, extra toppings 40p to 85p; prices include chips)

There were complaints about bitter cheese from all the children and some of them also found the meat in the hamburger rather greasy. Louise nominated the bacon burger as her favourite, though she thought they were all "excellent". This was not a universal opinion. There was general agreement that the hamburger was a bit boring but the bacon scored top marks.

STUDY TIP

One of the commonest and often most discouraging problems facing a student is not being able to understand a word or expression. It is important not to 'give up' because of isolated vocabulary comprehension problems. Remember, even in your own language you are very often faced with words you do not really understand, but this is rarely a major difficulty.

First of all, decide whether the word is important for grasping the meaning of the text and for the particular task you are carrying out. If it is, look for clues to meaning, either in the context or in the form of the word itself. In the context of an exam you may be able to answer a question if you can recognise the relevant information even without fully understanding it!

5 ☞ **What evidence is there in the introductory section for the following statements?**

1 People who bought McDonald's shares in 1965 made a lot of money.
2 Environmentalists are opposed to the development of burger restaurants.
3 McDonald's is popular in many countries because it represents American culture.
4 Environmentalists criticise fast foods because they create a lot of waste.
5 The children who participated in the test were not concerned about anything other than the quality of the burger.

Look back at the words and expressions you underlined in 4. Can you guess their meaning? You can use a dictionary to check.

6 ☞ **Find the following adjectives in the article. What features of the burgers are they used to praise or criticise?**

cold	boring	greasy	dry	tasty	bitter	rough
hard	soft	crispy	chewy	uncooked	salty	

Underline all the negative expressions used to describe the burgers.

7 ☞ **Answer the questions about sentences from the article.**

1 'The burgers were not top notch.' Were the burgers (a) not very good or (b) very good?
2 'Great expectations were on the whole fulfilled.' Were the children (a) disappointed by the burgers at McDonald's or (b) were they as good as they had expected?
3 'Ben praised the crispy vegetables.' Did he say something (a) positive or (b) negative about the vegetables?
4 'Louise couldn't deal with the Big Mac.' Did she (a) like or (b) dislike the Big Mac?

5 'Alex found the bread a bit chewy.' Did he (a) like or (b) dislike this
bread?

6 'George found the amount of vegetables overwhelming.' Were there
(a) too many or (b) not enough vegetables?

8 After reading the article, which fast-food restaurant would you choose to
eat at? Which would you avoid?

9 If you were buying one of the things below, what points would you
consider important? How would you get the necessary information and
how would you make your final choice?

a car   a computer   a camera   sports equipment   a dog

4 Transport

The aim of this unit is to focus on the following:

- predicting and forming an overall impression of a text
- skimming for main ideas
- looking for clues to text structure

The multiple-matching exam question requires you to match headings with paragraphs of the text.

Section A

1 The article below is about charter flights. Do you know what the difference is between a charter and a scheduled flight?
Write a few sentences about the particular features you associate with charter flights and those which you associate with scheduled flights? Think about the following features:

> reliability   comfort   cost   food   in-flight service
> business class   holiday travel   delays

2 ⚞ Look at the first five lines of the article. What do they suggest about the following?

a) the reputation of charter flights
b) the reality of today's charter standards

Is the article likely to be positive or negative about charter flights?

3 ⚞ Look quickly through the article and find out if it mentions the features listed in 1.

AIR CRAFT

DAVID WICKERS

Charter flights are traditionally considered a poor man's alternative to the scheduled carriers. But, after upgrading aeroplanes, service and destinations, all they need to develop is the image to reflect new higher standards.

| A | Unfair reputation |

What's the first thing that comes into your head when you hear the word "charter"? A bone-shaking ride on an airline you have never heard of? Nissen hut aerodromes? Kneecaps-under-the-chin seating? Survival rations? Flights to a handful of tacky destinations on the Med? Well, these days have gone; today, the charter flight has given way to a new species of holiday transport, the "leisure airline". Although still tainted by their old reputations, charter companies have been quietly bringing the quality of their services into line with the best of the scheduled carriers.

With new planes, smart interiors, charm-schooled staff, choice of menus, audio channels and films, world-wide destinations and even access to the big international airports, once the bastion of the schedules, they can no longer be dismissed as second class Singapore Airlines or the poor man's British Airways.

B

Take the planes. The charter airlines have invested enormous sums in new, quieter aircraft with all-weather flying capability (reducing the risks of delay or diversion). The oldest of the Airtours' fleet of eight MD 83 aircraft, for example, is 18 months. The age of Britain's newest airline fleet, Excalibur's three Airbus A320 aircraft, new on May 1, makes it the most modern in the world.

New planes are not just a matter of passenger well-being. They are more fuel-efficient, enabling airlines to sell seats to tour operators for less in real terms than 10 years ago. They are also more reliable; Airtours, for example, maintains that 98.9% of all its flights had "technical dispatch reliability", which translates as: no delay of more than 15 minutes due to technical reasons.

C

In-flight service on many, not all, charter airlines has improved beyond recognition. Since its launch in April 1987, Air 2000 has served 75 tons of smoked salmon, the equivalent to the take-off weight of an Airbus. On an Airtours flight, you'll be served a complimentary Buck's Fizz after take-off, while the children are busy with their special Kiddipacks, and all passengers are offered a choice of main course.

Fly on any Britannia service and the aircraft will be equipped with full in-flight video and 10-channel audio entertainment. On Caledonian you will be offered a choice of meal on flights of more than three hours, and in-flight entertainment on all.

D

The principal business of the charter airlines is holiday traffic. Ninety-five per cent of Thomson clients, for example, travel by charter. Each of the leading companies is either owned by a tour operator, or sired by the same parent company: Owner's Abroad, for example, owns Air 2000; Thomson/ Britannia; Cosmos/Monarch and, of course, Airtours/Airtours.

Despite these corporate ties, chartering is a highly competitive business. At present there are about 140 planes chasing a diminishing market. With prices forced down as low as they can go, one remaining field for competition is quality of service. The tour operators are well aware that it is the carrier that creates both the first and the last impression of the overall holiday. As Steve Allen, marketing director of Britannia, maintains: "To provide either a lousy start or an appalling end to a holiday costing £400 or £500 is utterly unacceptable."

E

Charter flights, therefore, have grown respectable in all but image. However, there are still shortcomings. If you are looking for the best in leg-room, fly scheduled. A charter airline makes money by packing in people. You lose between 1in and 2in of all the all-important seat pitch measured as the distance between headrests, compared with an economy seat on the better scheduled carriers.

F

Charter flights are also more likely to be delayed than scheduled flights. According to official figures, the average delay to a Gatwick charter recently was 43 minutes; the average delay to scheduled flights 18 minutes. Britannia maintains that 85% of its delays are the direct result of air traffic control problems. The destinations served by charters, typically in Spain, Italy and Greece, lie at the end of overcrowded airways which become notoriously congested during the peak summer months. Europe's skies are still governed by archaic technology. The personal computer used to write this article is more sophisticated than the equipment used to handle many European aircraft movements.

G

There is no business-class option on a charter flight. Many have tried, notably the now-defunct Air Europe, and some tour operators offer passengers the choice of an upgraded service; for an extra £50 or £60 you enjoy such perks as separate check-in, a better meal and a pass for the executive lounge at the airport, but none offers a business-class seat. Nor can you have the flexibility of an unrestricted ticket; fly on a charter and you come back the following week, or fortnight, with little room for manoeuvre.

H

But when it comes to price, the scheduled carriers are no match for the charters which fly according to loads, not timetables, and sell seats directly to tour operators. Their advertising costs are minimal by comparison. A flight costing £100 on a charter would cost up to twice the amount on a scheduled airline; fly to Australia and you could be paying as much as £500 more for the privilege.

4 Look carefully at the headings below and make notes against each heading on what you think the text says. Here are some words or expressions which you may find helpful.

fuel-efficient   new planes   choice of menus   quieter aircraft
smoked salmon   fewer delays   films   smart interiors
trained staff   children   free drinks   crowded airports

Non-stop flights
Comfort and reliability
Service and entertainment

EXAM TIP

The multiple-matching exam question opposite asks you to match headings with sections of an article. It is designed to test your ability to understand the main ideas expressed in a text. You are required to skim a large amount of text in a limited time. Don't attempt to read in great detail because you will probably not have time to finish the other questions on the Reading paper. And try not to let yourself be distracted by difficult vocabulary.

You may find the following step-by-step approach useful:

– study titles, layout, graphics and the questions for clues to general meaning
– skim through the text underlining key words
– match the more obvious headings
– for the less obvious answers, systematically identify key words
– finally, check that the headings you reject do not match any of the paragraphs

5 **🕰0** *Exam Question* For questions **1–7**, choose the most suitable heading for the various sections of the article from **A–J** below. One heading is given as an example. Try to do this question in no more than ten minutes.

1 Section B ☐	**A**	Delays
	B	Passenger survey
2 Section C ☐	**C**	Non-stop flights
3 Section D ☐	**D**	Cost
	E	Package deals
4 Section E ☐	**F**	Comfort and reliability
5 Section F ☐	**G**	Holiday business
	H	Available options
6 Section G ☐	**I**	Service and entertainment
7 Section H ☐	**J**	Seating space

6 **🕰0** Decide whether the following statements are true or false. Where they are incorrect decide what the article really says.

1 Nowadays most charter companies offer a quality of services better than scheduled carriers.
2 The modernisation of the charter carriers' aircraft fleet has helped keep holiday costs down.
3 The overseas holiday market is getting smaller.
4 There are more passengers on a charter flight than on the equivalent scheduled flight.
5 Many flight delays are due to out-of-date airport electronic equipment.
6 You can change the date of your return trip on a scheduled flight.
7 Charter companies offer a business option.
8 Charter advertising costs are very high.

7 **🕰0** Answer the questions about these words or expressions.

1 *bone-shaking ride:* Is this likely to be (a) an uncomfortable or (b) a comfortable flight?
2 *tacky destinations:* Are these likely to be (a) important and smart places or (b) small, little known places?
3 *lousy start:* Is this (a) a good or (b) a bad start?
4 *shortcomings:* Are charters as good as scheduled flights in all areas?
5 *archaic technology:* Is it likely to be (a) out-of-date or (b) modern?
6 *perks:* Are these (a) services offered to all passengers or (b) extras for those who pay a supplement?

Look through the article again and write down words you can use to talk about air travel.

8 If you had several options for the same destination, which of the points mentioned in the article would most influence your choice?

What form of transport do you most enjoy?

Section B

1 🔊 *Urban odyssey on a pedal and a prayer* is the title of the article in this section. Look carefully at the title and choose the description you think is closest to the likely content of the article:

a) The pleasures of cycling   c) The popularity of cycling
b) The dangers of cycling   d) Statistics about cycling

Which words in the title helped you to decide?

STUDY TIP

Before you read a text in detail you may want to *skim* through it to find out what it is about. To do this effectively the following strategies are useful:

— look at the title and graphics for clues to meaning
— identify important words as you go along
— focus on the opening sentences of paragraphs which often contain the main ideas

All these elements will help you build up an overall idea of the general meaning of the text.
You may find some texts easier to skim through than others. This may be because of the type of text you are dealing with. For example, it is usually more difficult to skim quickly through a text which suggests ideas indirectly rather than a straightforward informational text.

---

2 🔊 Skim quickly through the article and decide which of these photos was printed with the original article.

A

B

C

3 🔑 The first sentences of each paragraph of the article are printed below. Read the sentences to get an impression of the main ideas of the article. Some of the sentences contain words or expressions which give clues to how paragraphs are linked together. Look carefully at the sentences and underline the clues.

Example: a) <u>Another problem</u>: these words suggest that other problems have already been discussed in (a) previous paragraph(s).

a) Another problem is potholes.
b) Compared with much of the Continent, Britain has a low cycling casualty rate ...
c) But the main discomfort that would put me off becoming a full-time two-wheeling commuter is the pollution.
d) Cycle routes, some with specially paved-off and clearly marked tracks, are becoming more common, ...
e) The National Economic Development Office has just published a report comparing the status of cycling in different European countries.
f) It's not all bad though.
g) It is all a far cry from London, where only the brave, foolish or gas-masked couriers venture into the traffic.
h) But until those lazy motorists stop pumping heavy metals into cyclists' lungs, ...
i) The so-called green revolution has failed significantly to entice commuters out of their cars and on to bicycles in Britain's large cities.
j) A major problem is the driver who opens the car door into the street ...
k) There are cycle routes which, as far as possible, take bikes away from main road arteries into quieter streets.
l) Cambridge has a long tradition of cycles ruling the roads ...
m) However, I arrived shaken and nervous.
n) Early on in the cycling game you learn a few tricks.

Which sentence(s) could be the opening sentence of the article?

4 🔑 Think about the first sentences above and decide which you think are likely to introduce a paragraph which:

A presents cycling statistics
B describes the hazards of cycling in cities
C discusses what needs to be done in order to encourage people to cycle in cities

5 🔑 Read the article and match the first sentences with the paragraphs.

Urban odyssey on a pedal and a prayer

Sarah Lonsdale outstrips trains, buses and cars – but arrives shaken and half gassed

1 ... In smaller towns and cities where the roads are less congested and the journey to work shorter, cycling is less hazardous and more popular.

2 ... and it is the cyclists, rather than the drivers, who have an unofficial right of way. The cycling phenomenon in Cambridge, which is helped along by thousands of students and a flat landscape, has reached such heights that the local authority is trying to ban bicycles from the city centre.

3 ... Drivers turn into pigs and, despite efforts by some boroughs to mark out cycleways, accidents are common. In 1989, there were 28,941 reported accidents nationwide involving cycles. Of these, 294 were fatal – up 30 per cent on 1988 – and 4,836 resulted in serious injuries. Studies also show that 90 per cent of cycle casualties occur on busy main roads, 81 per cent of them in daylight.

4 ... I tried a route following streets recommended by the London Cycling Campaign from North Kensington to Waterloo Station, five miles away. I left at 9am and arrived at Waterloo at 9.35, beating car and tube travellers. And I was on a heavy, Thirties loop frame.

5 ... Even the most well-meaning motorist is unaware of bicycles and does not see them. On a roundabout, a learner pulled out into my path and I had to jam on the brakes while the poor man turned as white as a sheet. Silently cursing, I uncharitably hoped he would fail his test. The next time someone pulled out into my right of way I was not so silent and hurled a torrent of righteous anger at the culprit.

6 ... in the path of an oncoming cyclist, who is forced to swerve or perform a somersault over the door worthy of the most skilful circus clown.

7 ... Sitting behind smug, fat (you always imagine drivers are fat and unhealthy when you are on a bike) motorists pumping out lead and carbon monoxide, anger wells up inside you as you are forced to breathe in the noxious gases.

8 ... One is to stare down the driver who is pulling out in front of you. You get them right in the eyes, visually daring them to trespass across your path. A hard stare has averted many a near-death situation for me.

9 ... Many local authorities now operate a reimbursement policy and will pay out the cost of a new wheel if you can prove the damage was done by a pothole.

10 ... Cycling allows you to appreciate little important things that, cooped up in a car, you may never notice. In Ladbroke Road, I was assailed by the sights and smells of London waking up: strong coffee brewing in a streetside cafe, a florist carrying huge bunches of heady pink roses, a baker pumping out warm fresh bread steam. In Hyde Park, the ducks were going about their business, quacking and nodding as I passed.

11 ... as are special bicycle traffic lights. Many local authorities now have bicycle working parties which work with a town's cycling interests to plot the best routes.

12 ... In Switzerland, for example, the pharmaceuticals giant Ciba Geigy recently offered staff a free bicycle if they relinquished their car park parking space. The offer was taken up by 350 members of staff.

13 ... with 0.4 deaths per 100,000 of the population in the 15–99 age group. This compares with 2.1 per 100,000 in Belgium, 0.8 in France, 2.1 in the Netherlands and 1 in Ireland. Only Greece, with 0.2 deaths per 100,000 has a lower fatality rate.

14 ... turning us into an ingenious scrap-metal merchant's dream, then cycling will never become a favoured option to commuters, no matter how long they have to sit in their cars to get across town.

6 🔑 Answer the questions about these words or expressions:

1 *to jam on the brakes:* Did she brake (a) gently or (b) violently?
2 *to swerve:* the cyclist is forced to (a) fall off the bike or (b) avoid the car door
3 *wells up:* you become (a) more angry or (b) less angry
4 *noxious:* the exhaust gases (a) are harmful or (b) smell nasty
5 *cooped up:* Is this (a) a pleasant or (b) an unpleasant aspect of car travelling?

7 🔑 Find evidence in the article for the following statements. Where there is no evidence, decide what the article really says.

1 There are too many bicycles in Cambridge city centre.
2 Most accidents involving cyclists occur on main roads.
3 Cycling is a popular means of transport in London.
4 Bad driving is responsible for many accidents involving bicycles.
5 Cycling in a city can be very unhealthy.
6 Many local authorities are becoming more sensitive to the needs of cyclists.
7 Britain has the lowest European casualty rate.

8 Have you ever cycled in a town? If so, was your experience similar to that of the writer? Would you cycle again?

Do you think that encouraging cycling is the best answer to city traffic problems?

Travel

The aim of this unit is to focus on the following:

– scanning a text for specific information

– identifying relevant information to perform a task

The multiple-matching exam question requires you to match items of detail with places.

Section A

1 ⌐⊙ Look quickly at the text opposite and decide where you would expect to find it. What would you say the purpose of the text is? Choose from the following:

a) to inform readers of the interesting sights to be visited in China
b) to describe China
c) to sell holidays in China

2 ⌐⊙ Look through the description of the tour and trace it on the map below.

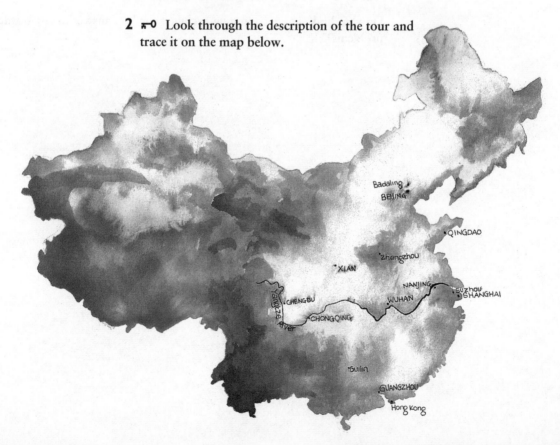

CHINA *the* BEAUTIFUL

22 nights from £2150.00

This journey encompasses many of the most impressive experiences of China, in an itinerary which varies from the northern stateliness of Beijing to the natural beauty of the Yangtse Gorges. We also visit the canal city of Suzhou famed for its gardens, the Terracotta Warriors of Xian and the marvellous scenery of Guilin, while in Chongqing, Shanghai and Wuhan we begin to piece together some of the aspects of China's modern history. For many, a highlight will be our journey along the Yangtse River, which cleaves its way through Sichuan Province and the famous Three Gorges, and on to the East China Plain.

For the first time, we have secured the exclusive use of the MS Kunlun, Chairman Mao's former private vessel on the mighty Yangtse river – the time-honoured route between Sichuan and the rest of China. The vessel will not only enable passengers to travel in comfort, accommodated in twin-berth cabins with en suite facilities, a restaurant, bar and on-board activities, but also ensure that they enjoy the many highlights of the river and the gorges in a journey over a leisurely, unrushed period – long enough to relax and capture the flavour of the Yangtse with selected and comprehensive on-shore visits.

Itinerary

Day 1 Depart afternoon, London Heathrow, on British Airways 747 to Beijing. **Day 2** Arrive Beijing and transfer to the hotel for 3-night stay. **Day 3** Beijing – Visit Tiananmen Square, with its early socialist architecture and in the afternoon visit the Forbidden City and Summer Palace, the former home to Chinese emperors. **Day 4** Beijing – Travel to Badaling, just 50 miles north of the city, to see the Great Wall of China. Return via the Ming Tombs. **Day 5** Beijing/Shanghai – fly to Shanghai, China's most populous city and a busy port. Stroll on the Bund overlooking Huangpu River with its backdrop of early 20th century buildings and visit the concession areas and the narrow streets of the old city. **Day 6** Shanghai/Suzhou – board the train for a short journey to the very charming town of Suzhou, famous for its silk and gardens. **Day 7** Suzhou/Nanjing via Wuxi on the Grand Canal – after breakfast board a canal boat. Stop at Wuxi on Lake Tai for lunch and continue journey to Nanjing. Stay in the city centre at Jinling Hotel. **Day 8** Nanjing/Yangtse Cruise – the pride of Nanjing is the river bridge spanning the Yangtse. Climb the many steps of Sun Yat Sen's mausoleum. In the afternoon board the MS Kunlun, Chairman Mao's private vessel, sail for Jiujiang. **Day 9** Yangtse Cruise – after a day's leisurely cruise, reach Jiujiang. Moor overnight. **Day 10** Yangtse Cruise – tour Lushan Mountain overlooking Lake Poyang and then continue the cruise towards Wuhan. **Day 11** Yangtse Cruise – reach Wuhan and tour the city. Visit Guiyuan Temple with its famous collection of statues, the Yangtse Bridge and East Lake. In the evening sail for Shashi and Jinzhou. **Day 12** Yangtse Cruise – disembark at Shashi in afternoon for an excursion to Jinzhou. Return to Kunlun. **Day 13** Yangtse Cruise – sail through first of the Three Gorges (Xiling), the longest at 75km. Reach Badong pre-midday, take in Da Ning River making on-shore visits to the dramatic Lesser Gorges. **Day 14** Yangtse River – Wanxian, pass through remaining two gorges (Wu and Qutang). **Day 15** arrive at Chongqing in the evening, and transfer to the hotel for an overnight stay. **Day 16** Chongqing/Xian, morning sightseeing then fly to Xian. Visit the museum and the Drum Tower. **Day 17** Xian/Qin Emperor's tomb – Lintong county's spectacular archaeological finds are now world famous. We will visit the site of the Terracotta Army, Huaqing Hot Springs and Ban Po village, a neolithic settlement. **Day 18** Xian/Guilin – fly to Guilin, considered one of China's most scenic areas. **Day 19** The Li River. One of the scenic highlights of a journey through China must be the river trip through the astonishing peaked scenery of Guilin, past bamboo groves, villages and solitary cormorant fishermen. We leave the vessel at Yangshuo and return to Guilin by bus. **Day 20** Guilin/Hong Kong – Visit some of the parks and the Reed Flute Caves before departure in evening for Hong Kong. On arrival transfer to a hotel for a two-night stay. **Day 21** Hong Kong – our representative will assist with local excursions and advise on shopping and eating out. **Day 22** Hong Kong – after a whole day enjoying attractions, we depart Hong Kong. Transfer to Kaitak Airport for the homeward British Airways (Boeing 747) flight. **Day 23** Arrive London Heathrow in the morning where our journey ends.

EXAM TIP

The multiple-matching exam question below asks you to match the items **1–15** with the answers **A–J**. There are usually one or more extra answers and some may be used more than once.

In this type of question you will need to look quickly through (*scan*) the text for specific information. The questions do not necessarily follow the order of the text.

This task is designed to test how quickly you can find information in a long text and the questions are usually fairly straightforward. Because you don't need to understand all the details, try not to waste too much time reading the whole text.

— Familiarise yourself with the questions.
— Scan the text, underlining relevant words and sentences as you go along.
— Check each answer by reading the information you have isolated.

3 **Exam Question** Use the extract from a travel brochure offering a holiday in China to match each of the sights **1–15** with one place chosen from the list **A–J**. It may not be necessary to use all the places in the list.

1	the Drum Tower	**A**	Badaling
2	a magnificent mausoleum	**B**	Suzhou
3	caves	**C**	Xian
4	a busy port	**D**	Shanghai
5	the former home of Chinese emperors	**E**	Nanjing
6	a temple containing a collection of statues	**F**	Guilin
7	scenic bamboo groves	**G**	Beijing
8	a neolithic settlement	**H**	Wuhan
9	hot springs	**I**	Hong Kong
10	cormorant fishermen	**J**	Wuxi
11	the Qin Emperor's tomb		
12	a square with early socialist architecture		
13	the Great Wall		
14	beautiful gardens		
15	silk workshops		

4 Does this type of holiday appeal to you? Write down three or four advantages and disadvantages of organised tours.

5 If you were organising a tour of your country, what itinerary would you suggest? List the sights and places you would visit. How would you travel?

Section B

1 When you visit a country it is useful to have a travel guide to help you
find the most interesting sights and deal with day-to-day practicalities.
Which of the following features do you find most useful in a guide book?

maps   useful addresses   accommodation information
cultural information   historical facts   walking itineraries
train timetables   restaurants   photographs   main sights
useful foreign phrases   information about the economy
advice for women travellers

2 The article which follows is from the book review section of a newspaper
and presents a selection of current travel guides.
Look quickly through the article and decide which guides best match the
priorities you chose in 1.

The world by chapter and verse

Frank Barrett conducts a grand tour around the bookshops for the best current travel guides

A Michelin Red Guides

If there is a better, more practical guide than the *Michelin Red Guide to France* (Michelin, £10.50), I have yet to find it. The wealth of symbols are initially hard to fathom, but decoding them is well worth the effort. There are good town-centre maps – now in colour – as well as brief guides to the main sights, the address of the local tourist office, local car dealers and much more.

There are other *Red Guides* to the Benelux countries, Germany, Spain & Portugal, Britain & Ireland and much more.

B Michelin Green Guides

The *Michelin Green Guides*, aimed at tourists, are a model of conciseness, presenting useful information in a user-friendly format. If I had to choose a favourite *Green Guide*, *Normandy* (Michelin, £5.95) is a perfect example of the genre, but there are more than 30 others covering the tourist regions of France as well as the main holiday destinations of Europe and North America.

C Cadogan Guides

The *Cadogan Guides* series has quickly grown to cover the most popular independent travel destinations from Australia, Bali and the Greek Islands to Tuscany & Umbria and Venice.

The latest in the series *Cadogan Guides: The Caribbean* (Cadogan Books, £12.95) by James Henderson, typifies the virtues of the books. Well presented, well researched and highly literate.

D The South American Handbook

It's possible that there is somebody somewhere who does not like *The South American Handbook* (Trade & Travel Publications, £19.95), but I have not yet met them. In terms of minute detail, excellent advice and encyclopaedic coverage it is the guide book against which all other guide books must measure themselves. The handbook has also spawned two offshoots concentrating on the Caribbean Islands and Central America.

E The Rough Guides

Originally aimed at the budget backpacker, the *Rough Guide* books are now written for all independent travellers. One of the most recent in the series, for example, *The Rough Guide to Nepal* (Harrap, £6.95) by David Reed is typically

---

STUDY TIP

The way you read depends on the type of text and your purpose for reading. You would not read a novel in the same way as a newspaper, or a bus timetable in the same way as an instruction leaflet, etc. When you are looking for some specific information – a train departure time on a station timetable or the football results in a newspaper – you run your eyes over or *scan* the text until you find what you are looking for. You do not attempt to read the whole text.

Before you scan a text you know what you are looking for. You therefore expect to find certain words. As you run your eyes over the text you identify and reject words which are important for meaning until you find what you want. You then focus on this part of the text only.

Many other clues help you in this process of finding what is relevant to your task: page layout, titles and headlines, graphics, typographical clues, etc.

comprehensive in coverage and authoritative in tone.

The series now covers most of the major travel destinations around the world: new titles include Poland, Czechoslovakia and Tuscany – there's also a guide for disabled travellers.

F *Blue Guides*

If you are trying to convince fellow travellers that you are a serious tourist, a *Blue Guide* effortlessly provides the right impression. They largely eschew the practicalities of travel to concentrate on questions of history, art and culture.

The *Blue Guide: France* (A&C Black, £14.95), for example, runs to almost 1,000 densely printed pages. Some people find the itinerary-based construction of the books irritating.

G *Lonely Planet*

Australia is the country responsible for producing the excellent and very extensive library of *Lonely Planet* books. The word "Bible" is rather over-used in descriptions of guide books, but it is appropriate for *South-East Asia on a Shoestring* (Lonely Planet, £9.95) by Tony Wheeler: the original *Lonely Planet* "yellow" guide first published in 1975.

H *Charming Small Hotel Guides*

A relative newcomer to the travel-publishing scene, but this small series of guides has quickly established itself as authoritative. *The Charming*

Small Hotel Guide to Italy (Duncan Petersen, £9.95), for example, succeeds in finding the best, most affordable hotels in the finest locations. The series also covers France, Great Britain and Spain.

I *Time Out Guides*

"Compact, honest, critical and opinionated" is how these guides describe themselves. It's a reasonable appraisal. *The Time Out Paris Guide* (Penguin, £7.99), for example, is an imaginative, practical guide to everything from politics to shopping. Guides in the series include London and New York.

J *Sunflower Books*

In the new age of "non-intrusive" tourism, the *Sunflower* books are the perfect travel guides. Covering a wide spread of European (and near-European) destinations, they concentrate on destination-friendly activities like walking.

K *The Independent Guide to Real Holidays Abroad*

This comprehensive travel guide would make a fine present for anyone interested in travel. The book lists information on more than 400 specialist holiday companies – as well as details about cheap air fares, courier flights, round-the-world tickets, tourist offices and other useful telephone numbers. The book is available in bookshops or direct from the publishers (£7.95).

3 ☞ **Which series would you choose if you wanted information on the following?**

1 shopping in New York
2 the history of Italy
3 a holiday with a disabled friend
4 a tour of monuments and museums
5 general travel information
6 cheap travel in south-east Asia
7 a wide variety of practical information, including town maps
8 booking a good, cheap hotel in Barcelona

4 Which guide would best suit your style of travelling?

5 🔊 The newspaper article below compares and discusses the merits of two of the guides mentioned above. Scan the text and decide which guides they are and what the journalist's attitude to them is.

The big guide divide

NOT LONG ago, on a remote Indonesian island, I came across a TV crew working on a secret project: shooting a pilot for the Lonely Planet TV series. I had stumbled upon what is to be the next front in the intensifying battle between the only two guides I automatically pick up whenever setting off on assignment: the Lonely Planet and the Rough Guides.

There are areas and subjects other guides do better. But otherwise there is no more consistent flow of information relevant to the practical needs of the independent traveller than that provided by these two series. Both are young and Green and were originally aimed at the budget traveller. Both manage to be oddly symmetrical even in their contrasting development.

Lonely Planet began in Australia 20 years ago and has recently published its 100th title. The Rough Guides started in Britain and last year notched up 50 titles in 10 years. Lonely Planet has the glossier product, could be said to be written by travellers who write (while the Rough Guides are by writers who travel), is strong on detail, reflects a certain uncomplicated Aussie "no worries" hedonism and originally concentrated on south-east Asia. The Rough Guides are stronger on culture and originally concentrated on Europe.

It is some years now since the two imprints started overlapping geographically, but now they have reached the point where each has its tanks smack in the middle of the other's lawn. Rough Guide has produced an award-winning guide to Thailand, long the opposition's best-selling title, and is now researching India and Australia – the other once seemingly unassailable jewels in the Lonely Planet's crown.

For its part, Lonely Planet has opened a UK office, launched its first western European titles, and is currently researching guides to Greece (subject of the first Rough Guide) and the UK itself. Both are now at pains to include the more affluent independent traveller in their readership, Lonely Planet rather more obviously so.

Both series wish to be seen occupying the moral high ground on matters of tourist pollution, and certainly I know from encounters with Lonely Planet writers in places yet unknown to mainstream tourists that these places will be ignored for their own good.

All that was missing until now was the Lonely Planet TV series. The Rough Guide one, in which Rough Guide itself now plays little part, is one reason why Lonely Planet, always dominant outside Europe, still has the lower profile in this country. Despite their rivalry, the two publishing houses are, of course, the best of friends and will not be drawn into mutual backbiting by mischievous journalists.

Mark Ottaway

6 🔑 Read quickly through the article and answer the questions:

  1 What type of travellers are the two series aimed at?
  2 What new category of travellers are they both trying to attract?
  3 What, according to the journalist, is the Australian (Aussie) outlook on life?
  4 How do these guides justify their 'moral' image?
  5 Which guide already has a TV series?

7 🔑 Find these expressions in the article and decide what the words *in italics* refer to. You can use a dictionary.

  1 '… the *next front* in the intensifying *battle* …'
  2 '… where *each* has its *tanks* smack in the middle of *the other's lawn*'
  3 'the other once seemingly unassailable *jewels* in the Lonely Planet's *crown*'

8 What countries would you most like to visit? How would you like to visit these countries? What particularly attracts you about them?
In general, what type of travelling most appeals to you?

6

Large-scale art

The aim of this unit is to focus on the following:

– forming an overall impression of a text and identifying the text type

– identifying clues to text structure

The 'gapped text' exam questions require you to reconstruct a text by inserting the missing sentences or paragraphs.

Section A

1 Look at the photograph of one of Christo's sculptures. Do you like it? Is it a 'work of art'?

2 🔑 The article in this section is incomplete. Look quickly through the 'gapped text' and answer the questions about text type.

1 What is the topic of the article?
2 Would you expect to find it in a newspaper or in an art magazine?

The fine art of disguise

THEO TROEV

CHRISTO JAVACHEFF, the Bulgarian sculptor renowned as an exponent of the new realism, was born in Sofia in 1935. Since 1958, he has been involved in a number of huge projects aimed both at dazzling people and making them conscious of the environment. These include wrapping the Pont Neuf in Paris, and a giant Valley Curtain which was erected in southern California in 1971.

1

"When I give lectures to western students who do not know what freedom is because they have been born free, I always emphasise that my art is a cry for freedom," he said.

2

His task was to help with the "artistic arrangement" of farms located along the route of the Old Orient Express. The students were ordered to arrange haystacks, trucks and tractors and paint buildings in such a way as to give foreign travellers on the train an image of prosperous communist agriculture.

3

According to Christo, the only difference between a socialist factory producing nothing but yellow clouds of smoke and one of his artistic wrappings is that the factory is financed by the tax-payer. Both produce more or less a symbolic reality – in both cases there is no economic effect, only a political or aesthetic one.

4

From there he went to Paris, where he spent almost ten years getting permission to wrap the Pont Neuf.

5

But things are different now. His work has been exhibited in Sofia and he was even invited to wrap the mausoleum in the capital's central square.

6

He used his commitments elsewhere as an excuse, but he seems deeply hurt by the fact that his fellow countrymen were afraid to stay in touch with him during the most difficult years of the Cold War.

A   In the early 1950s, Christo, then a 20-year-old student at the Sofia Fine Arts Academy, like all young Bulgarians had to spend part of his summer holidays on a state co-operative farm.

B   But Christo, who has not been home since his defection, declined.

C   Christo found the eastern bloc unsympathetic to modern art and, in 1957, he left for Austria, hidden in a cargo train.

D   He went back to Bulgaria to visit his family and former friends at the end of the Cold War, but he has decided not to return there to live.

E   Christo says it was the repressive Stalinist world of communist Bulgaria that first inspired his artistic vision of envelopment. He admits that had he not been born there, it would never have occurred to him to begin packaging his art.

F   This started the young artist thinking about the artistic value of landscapes and buildings viewed as something different from what they really were. While he was working at the co-operative farm he was creating illusions, transforming reality into Utopia.

G   In later years, when his name opened doors in New York, Paris, Berlin and London, he was still rarely mentioned in his native land.

EXAM TIP

The 'gapped' text question type is designed to test both your understanding of the text as a whole and of how text structure works.

The exam question below requires you to reconstruct the original text. In order to do this you first need to read through the article to identify the type of text you are dealing with – a writer developing an argument, a biography, a sequence of events, a description of a process, etc. You should have a clear understanding of what it is about and the way the writer develops the argument. Does it follow a chronological sequence? Does the writer develop his or her ideas in a logical order?

Here is a possible step-by-step routine for tackling this type of question when under exam pressure:

- Skim the 'gapped text' for text type and main ideas.
- Skim the paragraphs for main ideas, and underline words which are important for meaning.
- Make a tentative first choice.
- Look closely at each paragraph for structural clues and vocabulary links.
- Is the development of ideas logical? Read the whole text through and check the overall effect.

3 🎧 Read the 'gapped text' and the paragraphs and decide if the article does one or more of the following:

a) describes the life of the artist
b) discusses and comments on the artist's views

c) expresses the artist's views
d) expresses and explains the writer's views

4 🎧 *Exam Question* Read this newspaper article, then choose the best paragraph from **A–G** to fill each of the numbered gaps in the text. (There is one extra paragraph which does not belong in any of the gaps.) Try to do this question in no more than 15 minutes.

5 🎧 Check your answers by underlining words and ideas which help link paragraphs together. Are there any chronological clues in this text?

6 🎧 Answer the questions.

1 What first inspired Christo's artistic vision?
2 What does he describe as a 'cry for freedom'?
3 What started Christo thinking about the artistic value of landscapes and buildings viewed as something different from what they really are?
4 Why did Christo leave Bulgaria?
5 Where did he go after Austria?
6 How have attitudes to Christo's work changed in Bulgaria?
7 What did Christo 'decline'?
8 Why did he decline this invitation?

7 Do you known any other of Christo's works? Do you like his art? What would you like to see him wrap in the future?

Section B

1 The photo above shows an example of large-scale land art by the artist Simon English. How do you think the artist created this work?
Write down four or five words that you would use to describe the work in the photo.

2 ⚷ The magazine article about Simon English in this section is incomplete. Look quickly through the article and decide if it is mainly:

critical   argumentative   imaginative   descriptive

STUDY TIP

The sentences and paragraphs of a written text are not just 'lumped' together but are carefully ordered and linked in order to express the development of the writer's ideas. When you read in your own language you are not usually aware of text structure. However, you may find it useful to be able to recognise some of the structural devices used in text organisation, particularly when you are faced with a difficult text.

Most non-literary texts have a logical development:

– A writer will usually introduce a topic before discussing it, and words and expressions such as *moreover, however, but, on the other hand*, etc. will contrast, add to or qualify a previous argument.
– Some texts have a chronological development which is made clear with dates or time adverbs such as *after, then, next, later*, etc.

There are often grammatical clues:

– reference, e.g. the use of the definite article after the indefinite article; the use of pronouns to avoid repetition
– consistency of verb tenses

The big picture

PAUL SIEVEKING

Simon English always thought big. Several years ago when he was a fine arts student he started a series of works in which he wrote the names of things on the things themselves as a statement of the obvious. "I thought of writing 'universe' on the universe," he told the Salt Lake Tribune.

1

The following year he began to write "Earth" on the Earth, starting with a 2,000 kilometre long "E" across North America, marked out by 10 cairns (piles of stones) with explanatory plaques. Seven cairns are now complete, as well as two in South America plotting out the start of a vast "A". The remaining letters, "R, T, H" (across Africa, India and Australia) remain to be done, but he has the rest of his life to complete the word.

2

In the Eighties, English got involved in landscape gardening which inspired his first complete work. In 1989, he created a 200ft flying swan in a neighbour's field near Stratford-upon-Avon. "For four years I knew there was a swan figure in the camomile field, in the same way an artist can see a figure in a lump of stone or a block of wood," he said. "It was the most appropriate bird to be seen along the River Avon as the river flows alongside the sculpture."

3

"For these few midsummer days the swan shone white all day and gold at night," said the artist. "It was a joyful celebration of a hot and perfect English summer."

4

In 1990, the swan's "skeleton" could still be seen, lying in a scrub of daisies like the remains of an old flowerbed taken over by lawn. "I see gardening as a higher art form to balance shapes, colour and time," said English. "One can use time as a sculptural medium."

5

This negative image was reversed when the plastic was removed and the hay set on fire, turning it into ash. "It was an extremely powerful piece of work," Simon told the local newspaper. "It would be pompous to try and make these things permanent. They are not really transient, not when 20 million people can see them through the mass media. My greatest delight is hearing the ordinary person in the pub telling his mate all about it. It becomes part of the common culture, like a good joke."

6

The work was completed just in time to be filmed from the air by a Japanese television company. "Seen from the air they seem to be flying, hunting along the hedgerow," said the artist.

7

The brown wings were created from dead grass, the black spots from lime and sawdust, and the body from compost. The antennae and label were burnt into the grass with paraffin and sawdust. The image was still visible in April 1994.

8

This involves creating an image of a horse, a plough and a man, ploughed in the landscape in one day using a horse, a plough and a man. The image will be an acre in area, an acre being defined originally as the area ploughed by one man in one day.

3 🔁 Scan the article and paragraphs and find out which of the following points are mentioned. Try to do this in less than two minutes.

a) the artist's personal life
b) his childhood
c) where he works
d) artistic influences

e) a future project
f) the work in the photo above
g) the artist's comments on his work

A He mowed the field by hand for four days and nights. The figure was finished in time for the sun to rise directly over the swan's beak on a cloudless 21 June, Midsummer Day, and set over the left wing.

B In 1992, English created a zebra, 90 metres long and 70 metres high, to mark the last year when farmers were allowed to burn straw, a practice which leaves strips of black and yellow. After marking the shape, his team of volunteers raked the wet, ungathered straw into strips and laid black plastic between to bleach the grass.

C Simon English now lectures at Mid-Warwickshire College in Leamington. His landscape figures have been self-financed, although he has recently landed a grant of £1,000 from the West Midlands Arts Council for a project called "All in a Day's Work".

D Unfortunately, terrestrial technology couldn't match his vision. Instead, English hitch-hiked round England between June and September 1971 writing "England" in letters each measuring more than 40 miles in length (as seen from the air), marked out every 10 miles with 75 small flags. With each flag was an information sheet explaining the project, and a small map indicating the location of all the flags.

E "It wasn't simply a pretty picture. The swan was a cross-shape with the field as wing space. There was an axis point that went right through the middle. It was mathematically balanced, with the swan bisecting the field as the summer solstice bisects the year."

F Anonymous earth artists, over the centuries, have created large-scale figures in the landscape, many of which are still visible today. Simon English is keeping this age-old tradition alive with 200ft swans and giant zebras in the wheat fields of Britain.

G The composition for the summer of 1993 was a brown meadow butterfly, 250ft wide and an acre in area. It took three weeks in August to define the outline with sticks and tape and then mow the two-acre meadow.

H The artwork in January 1993 was two magpies with 300ft wingspans, entitled "Thieves of Time", on a field in Warwickshire. Magpies are traditionally associated with stealing: hence one of the birds holds "a bright object". The title also reflected the amount of time the project took to complete, what with the difficulty of the terrain and the dreadful weather.

I Like the ancient Nazca earth artists of the Peruvian high plateaux, Simon English creates shapes on the surface of the Earth to be seen from the air; when he was in Peru he met Dr Maria Reiche, who had spent many years studying the layout of the Nazca figures and pondering their significance. Here he learned something of the mechanics of large-scale land art.

4 🔑 Read the article and the paragraphs A–I and underline all the chronological clues which are likely to help you complete the passage.

5 🔑 *Exam Question* For questions **1–8**, you must choose which of the paragraphs **A–I** match the numbered gaps in the magazine article. There is one extra paragraph, which does not belong in any of the gaps.

6 🔊 Answer the questions about words and expressions from the article.

1 'Unfortunately, terrestrial technology couldn't match *his vision.*' What vision?
2 'He mowed *the field* by hand ...' What field?
3 '*The figure* was finished in time for the sun ...' What figure?
4 '*This negative image* was reversed when *the plastic was removed* ...' What image? Where was the plastic removed from?
5 '*The work* was completed just in time ...' Which work?
6 '*The image* was still visible in April 1994.' The image of what?
7 '*This* involves creating an image of a horse, ...' What does *This* refer to?

7 How do you feel about the non-permanent forms of art mentioned in this unit? Do you think this sort of art deserves to be taken seriously?

7

Children and education

The aim of this unit is to focus on the following:

– predicting main ideas from the title and introductions of a text
– identifying and interpreting opinions
– inferring information which is not clearly stated

The multiple-matching exam question requires you to match a statement expressing an opinion with the person who expressed it.

Section A

1 🔑 Look at the title and introduction of the newspaper article in this section and try to answer the questions.

1 What is the main topic of the article?
2 What does the introduction suggest is unusual about the teenagers who visit the camp in Florida?
3 What sort of information do you expect to read about in the article?

Now read the article and see if your predictions were right.

Teenagers in love (with money)

<u>Some kids go swimming, others prefer to play the stock market.</u> **Amon Cohen** visits a camp for trainee tycoons in Florida

IT IS 95 degrees in Palm Beach. Most sane teenagers are in pools or the Atlantic. But one small group of 11 to 15-year-olds in Nikes, T-shirts and baseball caps is sitting in a hotel conference room studying the Wall Street Journal.

They look up from their newspapers at a dark-suited supervisor. He asks: "Is it good that Ford is putting up its prices?" The teens are not sure. Could be good. Could be bad. Could be time for a swim.

"Yeah, it's good," the supervisor replies. "If they put up their prices, then profits go up and Ford can pay bigger dividends."

This wisdom is being imparted at The Breakers, one of the most exclusive hotels in the United States's most exclusive holiday resort, where the eighth annual Money Management Camp, a week-long course, is being run by Gruntal and Co, a New York stockbroking firm.

For a fee of $625 (£325, accommodation extra), the campers enjoy afternoon activities such as golf, volleyball and ice cream sundae parties; the morning schedule has such topics for consideration as "Ethics, Bonds, Mutual Funds", "Understanding Risks and Emotions" and "The Crash of '87".

The course is taught by Terry Upton, Gruntal Palm Beach's vice president and investments manager. Mr Upton, balding, sun-tanned and wearing a monogrammed shirt, admits to having been a pony-tailed socialist 20 years ago. Now he wears sober suits and is "a recognised authority on the subject of tax-exempt investments".

He is a good teacher. He does not patronise his pupils but whisks them through the jargon and mechanics of stock investment, answering questions clearly and firing off many himself.

One or two pupils stifle yawns, but most seem to be fascinated by the complexities of risk-reward analysis. As Mr Upton recites a litany of investors' maxims – "don't buy a company you don't

understand", "compound whenever you can afford to" – the kids scribble them down.

It would be nice to report that Mr Upton's pupils – 11 boys and four girls – are stereotypical spoilt American brats, but this is not the case. Confident, yes; acquisitive, yes; but almost all are friendly and modest.

The keenest tycoon among them is Gerard Di Santo II, from Rhode Island. Hugely affable, still carrying puppy fat at 13, he knows he is going to make a lot of money. Gerard already manages an imaginary portfolio in an investment game run by schools in his home state and helps his father, Gerard Di Santo I, with his property business.

"This is fun," he says. "It's good to learn about investment at a young age. I'm not bothered about being on the beach."

Keen as he is, the young investor does not intend to make the markets his main career: "I see it more as a hobby."

Gerard *père* approves. "The child is the father of the man. He likes business. I don't know if it is

2 🔑 Find these sentences in the article and answer the questions.

1 'Most sane teenagers are in pools or the Atlantic.' What does the writer seem to think about the kids on the course?

2 'He does not patronise his pupils but whisks them through the jargon and mechanics of stock investment, answering questions clearly and firing off many himself.' What is the writer's opinion of Mr Upton as a teacher?

lust for money but he pitches in all the time at work. Every American should look at the stock market. That is where their money comes from. The camp won't make children greedy. People are born to do more good than harm, and that carries into the stock market.

Also on the course is Christine McCann, 12, whose father, another Gerard, is assistant director of food and beverage at The Breakers. Christine, a diminutive girl with olive skin and dark hair in a pony-tail, does not look old enough to be worrying about boys, let alone fluctuations in Treasury bill prices.

She admits that "money is not one of my concerns right now" – her hobbies are "swimming, going to the beach, playing with friends and going to the mall".

Nevertheless, she already has serious plans, including an ambition to be a marine biologist, and her father reports that since the course started she has spent a couple of hours each day in his office going over the *WSJ*. Christine's seven-year-old sister is waiting enthusiastically for her chance to attend the camp, says Mr McCann. He does not believe that learning about investment is depriving her of her childhood. "Christine is a cheerleader," he says. "She does baby-sitting. She's an all-round American girl."

The occupations of the pupils' fathers vary from architect to hair stylist, but nearly all of them are self-made men.

Among them is Brad Culverhouse – father of John, 11 and uncle of Nicholas Ulmer, 12. Mr Culverhouse, from northern Florida, is an attorney, citrus fruit grower and cattle farmer. He earns $700,000 (£365,000) a year, yet he is a self-confessed "liberal" Democrat – which in the US is almost tantamount to membership of Militant. He sees no contradiction in sending his son to the camp – however liberal he is socially, he still believes in the power of investment.

"I believe in the trickle-down and the trickle-up theory," he says, explaining that if the poor become richer, they can spend more money to make the rich richer (and safer) as well.

On the last day of the camp, a limousine conveys the kids to the Gruntal office. The purpose of the visit is for the children to invest $100 each, included in the camp fee, in the stocks of their choice. Most of the children invest their "play money" in familiar names. Christine, for instance, opts for the Blockbuster video chains and Wendy's, a fast-food restaurant. Others go for Disney, Nike and Coca Cola.

But not Gerard Di Santo II. He has brought $1,000 in cash and is deliberating between two computer disc manufacturers he has researched, Western Digital and AMD. After consulting the Gruntal computer with one of the brokers on hand for the occasion, he settles on Western Digital as the better bet.

As Gerard departs, the broker comments: "That's a smart kid. He knew exactly why he wanted to buy that stock."

Gerard also wins the prize at the graduation banquet on the last night. And presenting the award, Mr Upton asks another of his rhetorical questions. "Is it bad to be a capitalist? No! It is if you gamble, but if you give some of your money to the poor, then it's OK."

Mr Upton stresses the need to honour gentlemen's agreements and warns the children off insider trading. But wider moral dilemmas, such as whether to invest in companies tearing up the rainforests or running mines in South Africa, are not on the agenda.

"It we are accused of being capitalists, that's fine because that is what we are. We are here to build wealth. There is nothing wrong with making money."

Gerard Di Santo II and his fellow campers would agree with that.

3 'It would be nice to report that Mr Upton's pupils are stereotypical spoilt American brats, but this is not the case.' Why is the writer disappointed?

4 'The camp won't make children greedy.' Who expresses this opinion?

5 'But wider moral dilemmas, such as whether to invest in companies tearing up the rainforests or running mines in South Africa, are not on the agenda.' Does the writer suggest that wider moral dilemmas should be on the agenda?

3 🔊 **The sentences (1–5) in 2 contain opinions which can be expressed more simply. Match the opinions with the reformulations.**

a) Mr Upton is an efficient teacher who treats the youngsters with respect.
b) They are very pleasant children.
c) Learning about investment does not have a bad effect on the children.
d) Normal youngsters would not choose to learn about investment during their holiday.
e) The pupils should be made aware of moral issues.

EXAM TIP

The exam question below asks you to match a statement expressing an opinion with the person who expressed it. Because you are told that the statements are opinions, you don't need to distinguish them from fact. But you do need to recognise the reformulation of the opinions. The opinions are not necessarily in the order in which they appear in the text. You may find the following steps useful:

– Read quickly through the text. Underline the names of the people listed in the question and the sentences expressing their opinions.
– Reread the opinions carefully.
– Match the opinions with the reformulations in the exam question.
– Match the reformulated opinions with the people who expressed them. Some of the opinions, especially those of the writer, may not always be clearly stated in the text, but suggested indirectly. For these questions you may find it helpful to think about the writer's attitude and the language he or she uses.

---

4 🔊 *Exam Question* Questions **1–9** consist of statements expressing the opinions of various people mentioned in the article. Choose the appropriate letter **A-G** to show which person expressed these opinions. (Some of the people expressed more than one view.) Try to do this question in no more than 15 minutes.

A The broker
B Amon Cohen
C Gerard Di Santo II
D Gerard Di Santo I
E Mr McCann
F Mr Culverhouse
G Mr Upton

1 All Americans should take an interest in the stock market. ☐
2 Capitalism is not a bad thing. ☐
3 A belief in social ideals is not contradictory to investment and earning money. ☐
4 Learning about investment is more fun than being on the beach. ☐
5 People are basically good and there is no reason why learning about money will make children bad. ☐
6 Gerard Di Santo II knows what he's doing. ☐
7 Learning about investment doesn't make children grow up too fast. ☐
8 Mr Upton is a good teacher. ☐
9 In business it is important to keep your word. ☐

5 Do you think the camp for trainee tycoons is a good idea? Write down three arguments in favour, three arguments against and your conclusion.

Section B

When you read a text you usually have a general idea of what it is about. It is only in very specific situations that you may be asked to read a text without any prior knowledge of its contents (in an examination, in a language class or the first chapter of a novel). It is useful to look carefully at titles and extract as much information as you can.

Many articles have a main title, as in the text you have just read: **Teenagers in love (with money)**. This suggests the main ideas of the article. There may also be a short sentence of introduction: **Some kids go swimming, others prefer to play the stock market. Amon Cohen visits a camp for trainee tycoons in Florida**. This is often a short explanation to hint at the main ideas and angle of the article.

Now that you have read the article in Section A, would you say the main heading and the introduction helped you form an overall impression?

Some articles also have extracts set in large or bold print or italics in the body of the text, like the text which follows. These may also give you an impression of the main ideas.

1 ☞ Look at the title of the article in this section and the extracts in italics and try to answer these questions.

1 What do you think the article is likely to be about?
2 What sort of people may have made the comments in italics?
3 What points do you think the article will make?

Now look quickly through the article and see if your predictions were right. Try not to spend more than five minutes doing this.

2 ☞ Read the article and decide who expressed the following opinions. What qualifies them to comment on the subject? Try to take no more than ten minutes.

1 We have a very good education system and we can cater for these children within it.
2 There are significant numbers of teachers who do not recognise the signs of giftedness.
3 Parents have other options besides withdrawal.
4 A lot of people worry about the social aspects of acceleration but a lot of these children are not enormously social whichever group you put them in.
5 It is better for them to stay in their age group and for the teacher to organise the curriculum to meet their needs.
6 Teaching should be to satisfy the needs of the child.

When teacher fails your infant prodigy

JUDITH JUDD

What is the best way to teach a genius? Britain's two youngest graduates for several hundred years – 13-year-olds Ruth Lawrence and Ganesh Sittampalam – achieved their success by markedly different routes. Ruth was taught at home by her father who then accompanied her to Oxford University where she studied full-time. Ganesh attended Surrey University at Guildford one day a week, continuing to follow the normal curriculum with classmates at King's College Junior School, Wimbledon. He still gained a first-class degree in two years. When his success was announced last month, the university said it was a landmark in the education of gifted children because he had not sacrificed his childhood for a degree.

"There is a climate of opinion in some schools that children of high ability can cope on their own."

Yet, according to the National Association for Gifted Children, many very able children suffer the same fate as Matthew Crippen when they attend school. They become bored, upset and regress. Dr Edward Chitham, the association's educational consultant, says: "There are significant numbers of teachers who do not recognise the signs of giftedness. The effect is that the child feels very alienated. There is a climate of opinion in some schools that children of high ability can cope on their own."

On the contrary, after five years at home with parents who have fostered their interest, the arrival at school where teachers have often not been trained to spot gifted children can be a shock. The association recently dealt with the case of a highly intelligent little boy who wrote very little because he worked out so much in his head. He was made to stay in at break to write down his ideas. Children who have a bad experience at school may suffer debilitating doubts about their ability despite the fact that they have every reason to be confident. So is the answer to take a child out of school and turn to an organisation like Education Otherwise, which helps home-educators of children with all abilities?

Mike Turner of the National Association for Curriculum Enrichment and Extension, opposes withdrawal. "We have a very good education system and we can cater for these children within it." His own school, St Anne's, Oldland, Bristol, a state primary, coped with a talented mathematician by inviting sixth formers from a local secondary school to come in and work at problem-solving with him. "We kept in close contact with his parents who felt a balanced personality was developing as well as an able mathematician." If we start taking the most able out of school, he says, we

3 ☞ The opinions in 2 have been reformulated below. Match the opinions with the reformulations. There are three extra reformulations.

a) Withdrawing a child from school is not the only solution.

b) Changing schools is often a good solution.

c) Special tuition in subjects like sport or music is difficult to provide within school hours.

d) Gifted children should not be moved out of their age group.

e) Many gifted children do not get on well with other children their own age.

f) Schools need to change their own view of gifted children.

g) The education system is well-adapted to the needs of all children.

h) Teachers should receive training to help them recognise and cope with gifted children.

i) Schools should adapt to the child's needs.

have to think about withdrawing the least able and any child who is exceptionally talented in one area of the curriculum, which could mean 40 per cent of the school population.

"The discipline and regimentation of some private schools is not right for a loner who wants to explore on his own."

Dr Chitham is also cautious: "We can support people who take their children out of school but our long-term aim is to try to change the climate of opinion in schools." Parents have other options besides withdrawal, he suggests. They can look around for a more suitable school. That may well be a state school with the right teacher and the right head. A fee-paying school is not necessarily the answer. "We get as many agonised calls from parents of children in private schools as we do from state school parents. The discipline and regimentation of some private schools is not right for a loner who wants to explore on his own." This is particularly true of primary schools. At secondary level, some fee-paying schools, with their greater resources, are able to offer a wider curriculum.

Rather than switching schools, parents can ask for their child to be put up a class, though experts disagree about the merits of "acceleration" and some schools and local authorities refuse to allow it. Mr Turner, who aims to spot and foster musical, sporting and artistic as well as academic ability in his school, says: "It is better for them to stay in their age group and for the teacher to organise the curriculum to meet their needs. It is not necessarily a question of giving them harder work, going on 10 exercises beyond everyone else, but of challenging them to higher and wider qualities of thought." In the case of sport or music, special provision may have to be made out of school.

"A lot of people worry about the social aspects of acceleration but a lot of these children are not enormously social whichever group you put them in."

Dr Chitham, however, says schools should be flexible about teaching children either full or part-time with an older group. Since able children do not always develop at the same rate in all subjects, they can be with an older group for maths, say, but with their own class most of the time. "A lot of people worry about the social aspects of acceleration but a lot of these children are not enormously social whichever group you put them in."

Many gifted children will progress cheerfully through school to a double first at university. Research by Joan Freeman of the European Council for High Ability suggests that a very able child is not necessarily a very difficult one. Dr Chitham advises that parents should remember that education is not a race and that children are not there to fulfil their parents' unfulfilled ambitions. Teaching should be to satisfy the needs of the child.

4 ⏻ Who holds the remaining opinions? How are they expressed in the article?

5 Read the article again and write down words you can use to talk about education. Which words can you use to describe your own education?

6 Do you think that children of all levels of ability should be taught together? Are all levels mixed together in schools in your country? Write a few sentences describing an argument for, an argument against and your conclusion.

The oceans

The aim of this unit is to focus on the following:

– identifying text type and the purpose of a text

– understanding main ideas

– dealing with difficult vocabulary

– evaluating a text and looking at the writer's style

The multiple-choice exam question requires you to choose the best of four options.

Section A

1 The newspaper article in this section is about how ocean currents influence the climate. Which of these words would you not expect to find in the article?

transfer	excitement	research	ice	invest	global
death	data	monitor	seabed	nightmare	tropics
topography	scientist	marvellous	direction		rescue
deep	helicopter	oceans	currents	equator	polar
warming	atmosphere	programme	executive		colder
minority	energy	climatic	valleys		

2 **Scan the text as quickly as possible to find where these ideas are mentioned. Try not to take more than five minutes.**

1 Deep ocean currents transfer heat from the equator to the polar regions.
2 Global warming has already caused significant changes to ocean currents.
3 A large number of countries are participating in a wide-scale research programme.
4 Ocean currents are essential factors in the planetary heat transfer system.
5 International research is aimed at a better understanding of climatic changes.
6 More data will be collected in this research initiative than ever before.
7 Research has shown that the topography of the seabed does not influence the direction of currents.
8 British scientists will monitor wind speeds in the polar regions.

3 ⌐o **Now read the article and decide whether the statements in 2 are true or false.**

EXAM TIP

The type of questions you will be asked about a text will depend largely on the type of text it is. Generally, scientific texts contain more facts than other types of material. The questions are therefore more likely to test detailed understanding rather than ability to infer what the writer means or to analyse the writer's style.

When you tackle a multiple-choice exam question like the one on page 61, if you don't immediately recognise the correct option or likely options, you may use a process of elimination. It's a good idea to establish a step-by-step approach, which may be especially useful when under pressure in an exam. You may find the following steps helpful:

– Read the whole text through once.
– Read all the questions and eliminate any options which are obviously incorrect.
– For each question, find the appropriate part of the text. Read this carefully and underline the relevant information.
– Choose the best option.
– At this stage you may still not be sure, so look for information which will eliminate one or other of the possible options.

Try not to read the whole text more than once. Train yourself to recognise and study only passages which are relevant to the questions.

Current accounts of the fate of the planet

Steve Connor on a vast sea search for clues to climate

In their darker moments, climatologists talk about their own "nightmare scenario". This is one where global warming has brought about such significant climatic changes that ocean currents change direction. One scene from the nightmare has the Gulf Stream moving south or even going into reverse, making winter in London look and feel like a St Petersburg January.

The ocean is a great moderating influence on the planet, soaking up heat around the tropics and depositing it in the cooler polar regions. Yet scientists know surprisingly little about how the sea does this – they estimate that the North Atlantic alone moves energy equivalent to the output of several hundred million power stations.

Last year oceanographers began their biggest international research initiative to learn more about ocean circulation. The first results from the World Ocean Circulation Experiment demonstrate just how complex the movement of sea water can be. They have also given scientists a glimpse of the amount of heat being exchanged between the oceans and the atmosphere. As part of the experiment, researchers are monitoring the speed and direction of ocean currents, water temperature and salinity.

Research ships taking part will gather detailed measurements at 24,000 points or "stations" along carefully designated trans-ocean routes. This undertaking dwarfs the 8,000 hydrographic stations created in the past hundred years of ocean surveying. A fleet of ships, buoys, seabed sensors and satellites will collect so much data that Britain, one of the 40 countries taking part,

has opened a research institute, the James Rennell Centre for Ocean Circulation in Southampton, to process them.

One of the justifications for the experiment, says John Woods, director of marine and atmospheric sciences at the Natural Environment Research Council, is that the oceans hold the key to understanding long-term changes in the global climate. The Earth has two "envelopes" – the ocean, consisting of slowly circulating water, and the atmosphere, made of fast-moving air. Far from being independent, they interact, one modifying the other until a balance is reached between them. The present balance came about at the end of the last Ice Age, about 10,000 years ago. Scientists hope that knowing more about the ocean's "weather patterns" will help them to predict climate changes further ahead.

Knowing how heat is moved around the ocean is crucial to such long-term forecasting. The top three metres of the ocean store more heat than all of the atmosphere. Some of the heat can be transported downward between 30 metres and several thousand metres. The deeper it goes, the longer it stays out of the atmosphere. Water heated in the equatorial region flows in shallow currents north or south towards the poles, where it releases its heat to the air and, as it becomes colder and denser, sinks to the sea floor, where it forms deep, cold currents that flow back to the equator.

John Gould, one of the British scientists taking part in the ocean circulation experiment, is discovering just how this occurs in the North Atlantic. Shallow currents, less than 500m deep, of warm water at about 8°C flow from the Atlantic into the Norwegian Sea, mainly along a path that follows the point where the continental shelf ends and the deep mid-ocean valleys begin. Meanwhile, at depths down to 5,000m, deep currents of cold water at about minus 1°C flow south into the Atlantic along the deep ocean valleys. (Salt water at this depth does not freeze at 0°C.)

Sensors positioned on the seabed have given Dr Gould and his researchers an accurate assessment of just how much cold water is flowing back into the North Atlantic having given up its heat to the atmosphere over north-west Europe. In total, he estimates, about 5 million cubic metres of water per second flows in these deep currents between Greenland and the British Isles. This means the warm water of the North Atlantic must be giving up about 200 million megawatts of energy to the atmosphere over north-west Europe.

Research at the other end of the world, in the seas around Antarctica, is also finding that sea-floor topography plays a crucial role in determining the direction of ocean currents. In the past, oceanographers have assumed, for instance, that surface currents such as the Gulf Stream do not extend much beyond a kilometre in depth. But an analysis of currents in Antarctic waters has shown that currents are not concentrated in the top kilometre, but reach down to the submerged mountain ranges.

Dr Woods believes such research will help to save lives. "More deaths can be prevented by ocean forecasting than by weather forecasting, and our economic and social well-being are more vulnerable to change in the ocean than in the atmosphere."

4 ⏻ *Exam Question*   There are a number of questions or unfinished sentences below. Choose the best answer from **A**, **B**, **C** or **D**.

1 Some scientists believe that global warming could
  A modify ocean currents.
  B change wind directions in the polar regions.
  C reduce the influence of currents.
  D increase wind speeds.

2 The first results have already confirmed
  A that heat is stocked at great depths.
  B that the last Ice Age ended about 10,000 years ago.
  C the complexity of ocean currents.
  D that Gulf Stream currents are situated in the surface layer of water.

3 Heat is transferred from the tropics to the poles
  A in the surface currents.
  B in the atmosphere.
  C in the deep currents.
  D along the seabed.

≫→

4 The atmosphere and the ocean
   A influence the climate independently.
   B interact and create a global climatic balance.
   C have no effect on the climate.
   D have only modified the climate since the last Ice Age.

5 Why is this research considered to be of great importance?
   A It will enable scientists of the future to prevent extreme climatic changes.
   B It will help scientists predict climate changes.
   C It unites a large number of different countries.
   D It will help dissipate the climatologists' 'nightmare scenario'.

5 ⌐○ Complete this summary without looking at the text. Use words from the list in 1.

Scientists believe that the oceans play a vital role in global climate regulation. Some climatologists fear that global .... could modify ocean .... and thus bring about drastic .... changes. The atmosphere and the .... interact on a planetary level until a climatic balance is reached. Shallow ocean currents transfer heat from the .... to the .... regions where it is released into the atmosphere. Deep, cold currents then flow back to the .... In a big international .... project, scientists are collecting vast amounts of .... in the 24,000 different stations placed on strategic ocean routes. The first available results from the North Atlantic show that shallow, warm currents follow the edge of the continental shelf and the deep, cold currents flow along ocean .... at depths of around 5,000m. These currents transfer enormous quantities of .... to the North Atlantic. Research in the Antarctic has found that .... topography is vital in determining the .... of ocean currents.

6 Scientific texts often look more complicated than they really are. Look at the article in this section again and note down any 'difficult' scientific words or expressions.

7 What do you know about global warming?
The opening sentence of the text suggests that there are other 'nightmare scenarios'. What scenarios is the writer probably referring to?

Section B

1 ⌐0 The extracts below are the opening paragraphs of two different articles on the same subject which appeared in different magazines. Read the extracts and answer the questions.

1 What is the subject of the articles?
2 Find four facts which both articles mention.
3 Find one fact which is different in the two articles.
4 What images are used in the texts to describe the shoes? What particular effect does the image in B have?
5 What does the first paragraph of A suggest about the rest of the article?

A

Flotsam footwear

Serendipity often comes to the aid of science. An amateur astronomer spots a nova, a fisherman captures a coelacanth in his net, a pair of oceanographers map the ocean currents by monitoring the advance of an accidental shoe spill ...

A shoe spill? On May 27, 1990, a freighter was buffeted by a severe gale in the north-east Pacific Ocean, and five shipping containers of Nike footgear went over the side. Like a fleet of message-bearing bottles, the 80,000 sneakers began washing ashore in British Columbia, Washington and Oregon in early 1991.

B

Nike's sole survivors hit the beaches

For the past 18 months, a Japanese armada has been sailing silently across the Pacific. Now, these secret invaders have begun to infiltrate the shores of the United States. The explanation for the invasion is pedestrian, quite literally, for the flotilla is made up of 40,000 Nike trainers which have been slowly bobbing around the Pacific Ocean since the spring of 1990.

2 ⌐0 Without reading the texts in detail, match the first paragraphs with the rest of the articles.

3 ⌐0 The two articles are reporting exactly the same incident but the emphasis is different. The most obvious point is the difference in emphasis on the scientific aspect. Scan the two texts and decide which one focuses most on this aspect. What comments can you make about:

– length of text devoted to scientific aspect
– vocabulary and descriptions
– reference to people
– use of quotations

Text 1

News that these sartorial requisites have met a watery fate may dismay the youth of the West. However, it has brought joy to Oregon's beachcombers, who have been making a fortune reselling the trainers which, bizarrely, have survived their briny immersion with surprising resilience. Odder still, the data provided by plotting the Nike armada's progress has allowed oceanographers to test several complex theories about the detailed mechanics of Pacific currents. 'It has been a real bonus to our work,' said James Ingraham, of the US National Marine Fisheries Service.

This strange story began on 27 May 1990, when a storm struck the freighter Hansa Carrier, which was en route from Korea to the US. The ship survived, but its shipment of Nike trainers was washed overboard. Not a sole was saved. The incident was forgotten until November that year, when Nike trainers began appearing along the shores of Oregon. Large hiking boots, high-top trainers and loafers began to bob landwards at first in ones and twos, then in scores, eventually in their thousands. To the incredulity of locals, the beaches were swamped with multicoloured trainers. Within weeks, this well-heeled landing army had created a thriving new local economy. Beachcombers held 'swap-meets' where they exchanged right and left shoes, which they then resold in pairs.

'I got my pair for $20,' said Dr Ingraham. 'That's about a quarter of the price I would have paid in a store. Admittedly they had spent a year sloshing about the Pacific, but after I'd worn them a couple of times they loosened up and are quite comfortable now.' The fact that their trainers were still wearable after many months' battering by storms and water would suggest Nike products have a certain weather-proofing prowess, a quality that could well be marketed. However, this has not been seized upon.

'We contacted Nike, but they didn't want to know,' said Dr Ingraham. 'Maybe a beachcomber's recommendation is not quite the testimony that Nike were seeking.' Maybe not, but the longevity of the trainers has been a real boost for Dr Ingraham who, with colleague Dr Curtis Ebbesmeyer, began studying the shoes' oceanographic peregrinations. They used the data to produce a lengthy paper for the Transactions of the American Geophysical Union. They report that many of the shoes appeared further south than would normally have been expected for flotsam borne by the tropical Pacific currents that head northwards to Alaska. Now, as the currents have swept back out to sea from Oregon, the shoes have been heading southwards and eastwards, and already some have appeared on the shores of Hawaii.

'The next stop is Japan,' added Dr Ingraham. It brings a whole new meaning to the idea of circuit training …

Robin McKie

STUDY TIP

A writer can say the same thing in many different ways. The way he or she chooses to write will not only depend on personal style but also on the type of text. For example, a scientific report on nuclear physics in a general interest magazine is likely to be interesting and enjoyable to read because it presents main ideas and avoids excessive detail. An article on the same topic in a specialists' journal will probably be full of complicated details which will only be of interest to a physicist. The purpose of the general interest article is to interest and inform a large number of readers; it should be attractive and not too difficult to read. The purpose of the specialist article is to report and analyse facts; it should be clear and concise.

When you open a newspaper or magazine you already have a good idea of the type of text you will find in it. However, when faced with a text out of context it may be helpful to ask the following questions:

- What is the topic of the text?   – Who is it for?
- Where would it appear?   – What is the purpose of the text?

Text 2

When Curtis C. Ebbesmeyer of Evans-Hamilton, a marine instruments company in Seattle, and W. James Ingraham, Jr, of the National Marine Fisheries Service heard news reports of the shoe spill, they immediately realised they had stumbled across a potentially useful ocean drift experiment. 'I tried to find the scientists who were tracking down the shoes, but nobody was,' Ebbesmeyer recalls. 'It surprised me.'

Ebbesmeyer contacted his friend Ingraham, who monitors surface currents to determine their effects on salmon migration. With the eager assistance of a network of beachcombers, the researchers recovered about 1,300 of the shoes. Because the location of the spill was well-known, the peripatetic shoes could provide a calibration point for computer models of ocean surface currents.

Ingraham then ran a computer hindcast to retrace the path of the shoes. It was a 'perfect little get-together,' as he describes it. His model showed that the 1990 path of drift was much farther south than usual. In certain other years, such as 1982, ocean currents associated with warm water in the tropical Pacific would have caused most of the shoes to drift toward Alaska.

The scientific value of the spill has by no means dried up. Some of the shoes recently reached Hawaii, and others 'should be reaching Japan shortly,' Ebbesmeyer notes. Any additional shoes that wash ashore will help the researchers as they expand their study of ocean surface drift to the Western Pacific.

The great shoe spill of 1990 has also had some practical effects. Artist Steve McLeod of Oregon has earned $568 by collecting and selling the seafaring footwear. And both Ebbesmeyer and Ingraham are sporting their own recovered Nikes. Ebbesmeyer recommends giving the shoes a hot-water wash before wearing them; a long period of drifting may be good for science, but it is bad for comfort. 'The shoes are real stiff after two years in the ocean,' he reports.

Corey S. Powell

4 🔑 Scan Text 1 and find answers to the following questions in less than five minutes.

1 What have beachcombers been doing with the trainers?
2 What happened to the ship which was carrying the cargo of trainers?
3 Where were the first shoes washed ashore?
4 Why was this destination surprising?
5 How did Nike react to the fact that the trainers could still be worn after months in the sea?

Are the points above mentioned in Text 2? If so, what are the main differences in their presentation?

5 🔑 In what sort of magazine or newspaper would you expect to find these articles?

a) a general science magazine
b) a specialist journal
c) a daily newspaper

What helped you make up your mind?

6 Which text do you find the most difficult and which the most interesting to read? Which do you think is the better report on the shoe incident?

7 Have you ever had a 'lucky find'? Write a few lines describing what you found and what you did.

Memorable incidents

The aim of this unit is to focus on the following:

– forming an overall impression of a text and identifying the text type

– interpreting the purpose of sentences in a text

– identifying clues to text structure

The 'gapped text' exam questions require you to reconstruct a text by inserting the missing paragraphs.

Section A

1 ↗○ Look quickly through the newspaper article below. Which word would you use to describe the type of passage?

descriptive   informational   narrative   opinion

2 ↗○ Scan the incomplete passage and paragraphs and answer these general questions.

1 What is the main idea of the passage?
2 Where does the event take place?
3 How many people are mentioned? Who are they?
4 What happens?
5 What is the outcome of the story?

This stiff grey fin was moving purposefully towards us ...

RICHARD E. GRANT TALKS TO DANNY DANZIGER

WHEN I was eight, my parents, my younger brother, Stewart, and a girl called Margo Edwards, who was at school with us, went on holiday to Mozambique. One day, we took out a small rowing boat with an outboard motor on it, and went fishing on this vast lagoon at a place called San Martina.

> **1**

Suddenly, as if out of nowhere, there was this disturbance in the water. I remember everyone initially thought it was a dolphin, but it wasn't leaping in and out of the water, and before long we could see this stiff grey fin moving purposefully towards us.

It then circled around our rowing boat, and I remember my father saying: "Well, I think that's a shark ..."

> **2**

My mother was screaming, and father was shouting obscenities at this thing, which he was trying to bash back with one of his oars. I had never seen my parents in obvious terror before, and that's something which never leaves you.

3

My mother clutched the three of us around her. I remember she had a voluminous navy blue towelling robe, with huge starfishes and sunflowers on it, and us three kids gratefully huddled together inside it.

4

As soon as we were in the fishing boat there was this almost hysterical laughter, and I remember feeling very cold, and being unable to stop shivering.

5

We all talked about it incessantly, too, and probably made out we were far braver than we were. And there was lots of re-enactment, I remember that we made mud pools, one of us would be crawling along playing the shark, and the others screaming and shouting: "Kill the shark!"

6

We all touched it. There's no texture quite like a shark; its skin is very abrasive, like leather with steel wool attached to it. If you ran your hand hard against it, you would suffer the equivalent of stinging nettles.

7

I suppose I do go on about it. I'll come across friends I haven't seen for 20 years, and the first thing they'll say is: "Still going on about that shark?" So I think it must have really affected me. I've never since had a closer sense of feeling I was going to die, and so theatre critics, job rejection, everything else daunting in life seems less frightening in relation to that.

A   For the longest time this thing kept circling around us, and ramming our rowing boat, while Dad continued fending it off, stabbing at it with his oar, which was probably the worst thing to have done because it must have made the beast even more livid than it already was.

B   Our story went back to the town, it spread like wildfire, everybody knew about it, and people talked about it endlessly. My father was regarded as a bit of a hero: Dad the sharkbasher. If he'd caught the thing, then I suppose he would have been completely heroic.

C   My daughter likes to hear this story a lot. She's five now, so she likes monstrous or horrific tales. She hasn't seen the film *Jaws*, I'm keeping that for a few years' hence – besides, I nearly had a thrombosis when I saw *Jaws* – that grey fin moving relentlessly through the water, coming towards you …

D   It was early evening when the motor broke down, and we were stranded. We started to shout in the hope that somebody would hear us; we knew the sound could travel because of the water being very flat and calm.

E   Two or three weeks later, near the end of our holiday, the shark was caught by one of the local fishermen, and put in the main square for people to go and see. The thing was strung up on a pole, and it looked horrific because they had slit its stomach open, all its innards had fallen out, and all the intestines were lying in a pile underneath it, with flies buzzing around. Everybody came to see it, and people took pictures.

F   The shark became a legend in the town and there were many local fishermen who claimed to have seen it prowling around the bay. But despite all the stories of sightings, nobody ever managed to catch the thing.

G   And then this monster started bashing our boat, which began rocking from side to side, and everyone got hysterical. We were just terrified because the boat was by now rocking so much we thought we were going to be tipped into the water and chomped up by this thing. I remember assuming that we were going to die.

H   Eventually, people in a fishing boat heard us screaming, and came alongside, and a fisherman tied our boat up to his. He was very careful, or he seemed to be, and he and my father handed first us kids, and then my mother, through to his boat, and our rowing boat was towed behind.

EXAM TIP

If the 'gapped' text is a story, as in the exam question here, you may find it helpful, as you read the passage for the first time, to ask yourself general questions about the story. As you read, remember to underline the reference words and time markers. These will help you to recognise the links between paragraphs when you look more closely at the structure of the passage.

3 Now read the passage carefully and underline the reference words and time markers. Check your answers to the questions in 2 as you read.

4 ☞ *Exam Question*   Read the article, then choose the best paragraph from **A–H** to fill each of the numbered gaps in the text. (There is one extra paragraph which does not belong in any of the gaps.) Try to do this question in no more than 15 minutes.

5 ☞ Find these sentences in the passage. What do the words or expressions which are *in italics* refer to?

1 '… father was shouting obscenities at *this thing*,…'
2 'My mother clutched *the three of us* around her.'
3 '… we were in *the fishing boat* …'
4 'We all talked about *it* …'
5 'We all touched *it*.'
6 'I do go on about *it*.'
7 '… *this thing* kept circling …'
8 'My daughter likes to hear *this story* a lot.'
9 '… when *the motor* broke down, …'
10 'And *then this monster* started bashing …'

6 Can you remember a frightening experience? Write a paragraph describing what happened and how you felt at the time. How do you feel about the incident today?

Section B

1 🔑 The passage in this section is an extract from *Honkytonk Gelato* by the travel writer Stephen Brook. Look quickly through the incomplete passage and paragraphs and answer the questions. Try not to take more than five minutes.

1 What incident does the passage relate?
2 Where does it take place?
3 What is the outcome at the end of this passage?

STUDY TIP

When a writer relates an incident or tells a story he or she usually includes in the text more than just the 'bare bones' of the story itself. He or she will probably comment on what happens, give explanations and describe people, places and feelings. When you are trying to complete a 'gapped' text you may find it useful to distinguish between sentences which describe the action and those which comment on events. This may help you follow the thread of the story.

---

2 🔑 The writer tells his story and comments on what happens and on his feelings. Find these sentences in the passage. Tick the sentences which describe the action and put a cross by those which are comments.

1 'He went away.'
2 ' "That was not smart ..." '
3 '... but my hammering roused the hotel clerk.'
4 'One of those cars, bumping towards the Main Street exit could well have my property ...'
5 '... I spotted two items that the thieves had missed.'
6 'It was therefore painfully evident that the motel had no security ...'
7 '... it must have been a joy to rob me, ...'
8 '... the youth got out of his car and opened the boot.'
9 'I strode towards the motel office.'
10 'It seemed distinctly possible that with no notes, ...'
11 'After half an hour the police arrived.'
12 'The next motorist I stopped was less co-operative.'

3 Underline more phrases and sentences in the passage which describe the action.

4 🔑 *Exam Question*   Read the extract from a travel book then choose the best section from **A–H** to fill each of the numbered gaps in the text. (There is one extra section which does not belong in any of the gaps.)

5 🔑 Find words and expressions in the passage which describe the writer's feelings.

A Hitch

TO BE exact: all my clothes, my typewriter, my passport and driving licence, my diaries, notebooks, address book, house keys, a few hundred photographs and negatives, and a large amount of cash. Even my razor and toothbrush had gone, and the book I'd left lying open on the bed when I'd gone out. All that remained were a few items I kept in the car, and my credit cards which I was carrying with me.

1

I strode towards the motel office. Again I passed the loitering girls. They were silent, motionless. It seemed obvious to me that they knew what had happened. The office was locked – it was after midnight – but my hammering roused the night clerk.

2

Checking the room once more, I spotted two items that the thieves had missed. Indeed, they were of no value, except to me. One was the notebook from which I'd typed up the stolen notes. That meant that I could in theory reconstruct much of what had been lost. Secondly, a blue folder in which I'd thrown the addresses and phone numbers of every single contact I'd made or would be making in Texas. It dawned on me that if I could rewrite my notes, get my hands on some more money, and replace some clothes, I could continue after all.

3

Another fifteen minutes went by. Just to sit in that room depressed me, so I went out and paced up and down the forecourt. Even at such a late hour the place was humming, and it didn't take long to realise that the motel fulfilled a very different function at night from that of resthouse for the road-weary. Large battered sedans drove in and out. Pairs of men sat quietly in darkened cars, talking, watching. One of those cars, bumping towards the Main Street exit, could well have my property stowed in its boot. The thought was intolerable, so the next time I saw a car making for the exit, I stepped out and flagged it down.

4

To which pretty speech the driver replied: "Hey man, you're crazy. You think I got your stuff? That's crazy man. I don't want you givin' no number to the police. I ain't got your stuff but this car – well, I just don't want you giving out no number."

Shaking his head in disbelief, the youth got out of his car and opened the boot. Tyres, toolbox, comic books. No suitcases. I apologised for bothering him and, muttering, he drove off.

5

After half an hour the police arrived. I explained what had happened. They nodded, made notes; they'd heard similar stories too often before. "It's real tough, something like this happening your first night in the city, but can I ask you something?"

"Of course."

"What are you doing staying in a whorehouse?"

6

"Think I'll get my stuff back?" I plaintively asked the police.

"You'll never see it again. Maybe they'll throw your papers and those notes you're so anxious about into a dump truck or a pile of trash near the road. You could check 'em in the morning. But my guess is you won't see your clothes again unless you check out every flea market in Houston."

7

"That was not smart," said the horrified cop. "If you'd stopped the guy who had your stuff, he'd probably have shot your face off. They shoot first round here."

6 🔊 **What does the passage tell us about the following people's reactions?**

- the clerk
- the security man
- the first driver
- the second driver
- the cop

A   There was a flashing light outside my door, then a knock. Not the police, but a security man employed by the hotel. I told him what had occurred; he was sympathetic, until I pointed out that his visit and his concern came rather late in the day. The motel, I said, had some cheek sending round their security man, since my room, situated on the ground floor and facing the main forecourt, had not been broken into but had been entered with a key. It was therefore painfully evident that the motel had no security to speak of. He went away.

B   The next motorist I stopped was less co-operative. He refused absolutely to let me search his car. I didn't argue. He was with a girl, and it was unlikely he'd back down in front of her. Off he went, and I jotted down the number. It began to occur to me I wasn't getting anywhere.

C   "I did try searching some cars that were leaving the motel."
"You what?" he said.
I explained how I'd flagged down vehicles and attempted to search them.

D   "Excuse me," I said politely as the driver, bemused, lowered his window, "but I've just been robbed at this motel and am anxious to recover my possessions. Now I've no right to ask this, but I'd like to inspect your car. It's not that I suspect you, it's just that I suspect everybody. You're perfectly at liberty to refuse, but I should tell you that I've noted your licence number and if you refuse to let me look inside your car, I shall pass it on to the police."

E   I indulged in some therapeutic yelling and ordered him to call the police. Then I marched back to my empty room, where I tried to calm myself. Two feelings were paramount: the sense of outrage, violation, that anyone who has been robbed experiences, and a sickening desolation at the thought that almost a month's notes had been stashed in one of the stolen cases. It seemed distinctly possible that with no notes, no money, no photographs, and no clothes, I would have to abandon the journey.

F   I woke two hours later, got up early to begin an exciting day that consisted mostly of searching rubbish dumps and checking pawn shops. I bought myself a razor so I could at least shave, and moved to another motel.

G   Since I hadn't unpacked much, it must have been a joy to rob me, and I could picture the thieves scarcely able to believe their luck as they simply picked up my bulging cases and carried them away. It couldn't have taken them more than a minute to wipe me out.

H   "How was I to know this is a whorehouse? It's obvious now, but when I checked in this afternoon in broad daylight it looked like any other cheap motel. How could I tell?"
"Because every motel on Main Street is a whorehouse."
"I didn't know that. They don't tell you that in the brochures your tourist offices hand out."

7 Have you ever had anything stolen from you? If so, write a paragraph describing the incident. How did you feel? What did you do?
If not, how do you think you would react? What is the most precious thing you own? How do you keep it safe? Are you careful with your property?
When you travel, how do you keep your property or your money safe?

10

Cultural issues

The aim of this unit is to focus on the following:

– scanning for specific information

– inferring a writer's opinions from the way he or she expresses him or herself

– evaluating the text

The multiple-matching exam questions require you to complete sentences with phrases.

Section A

1 🔊 The three articles in this section are about three different languages. Look quickly at the articles and decide what languages they are about. What do two of the languages have in common? Try not to take more than one minute.

Text 1

FRANCIS FAVEREAU is still reeling from the success of his Breton-French dictionary. With only 200 copies of an initial print-run of 1,700 left on the shelves, the 1.9 kg tome – the largest of its kind – is fast selling out and publishers Skol Vreizh are gearing up for a second run.

For a language that has long been considered "threatened" – it was banned in public for most of the 19th century and was given only partial recognition as late as 1951 – the dictionary has been widely welcomed.

First to order copies of *Geriadur Meur brezhoneg ar vreman* were the region's 22 bilingual "immersion" schools, where children are taught solely in Breton until the age of eight, after which they learn in both languages.

Now a pocket-size Petit Favereau is being edited for publication at the end of the year. Between 600,000 and 700,000 people out of the region's two million-strong population understand Breton. As many as 200,000 people speak it daily.

According to Favereau: "There is a decline in the number of people speaking Breton in their daily lives because of the demise of traditional speakers, but there is a massive resurgence of Breton sentiment and interest in the language and culture."

Favereau puts this down to an increase in the number of "new Bretons" – people who as children were not taught the language but want their offspring to learn it. Some 80 per cent of Bretons are in favour of the language being taught in all Brittany's schools. Parents have even gone on a hunger strike

in their efforts to get Breton put on the curriculum.

Mounting frustration and anger felt by many Bretons reached a peak last year when the French government joined the British in refusing to sign the European Charter for Regional Languages, thus reaffirming French as France's only legal language.

The massive Yes vote that Bretons bestowed on Europe in the Maastricht referendum bears sharp testimony to the belief that a united Europe will give the region the boost it so desperately needs by providing money for cultural projects. Europe's minority languages will receive an Ecu3.5 million grant from the European Commission this year.

Julie Read, Melanie Wright and Isabel Conway

Text 2

THE SURVIVAL of Frisian, spoken by about 300,000 of the Netherlands' 15 million inhabi-tants, is under increasing threat because Dutch itself, as a minority European language, may even

be fighting for its life.

Yet within the northern province of Friesland there is a

strong sense of pride in the language which underlines the region's distinct cultural identity.

The Frisians have been vocal in their demands for the retention of their independence and their own language. A well-defined Frisian movement continues to push for state recognition, the money to pursue educational and cultural goals, and a more official status for their language.

They have had mixed success. An important victory in 1980 was the introduction of compulsory Frisian in primary schools.

However, Geske Krol-Benedictus, a leading member of the Frisian National Party, points out: "Often the standard of teaching is poor and it depends completely on the individual commitment of the teacher."

Only five per cent of secondary level students take Frisian as a subject and few of those who speak Frisian can read or write it.

Nevertheless, the majority of Frisians want the language to occupy a position equal to that of Dutch in both administrative and judicial matters.

The scant attention the Dutch national media pays to Frisian is a continuing source of irritation. On the infrequent occasions when Frisian is spoken on Dutch television it is accompanied by subtitles. The regional Friesland radio network provides 20 hours' broadcasting each week and the main newspapers in the province, the *Friesch Daglad* and the *Leeuwarder Courant*, publish only a single Frisian paper each week.

Julie Read, Melanie Wright
and Isabel Conway

Text 3

LIKE it or not, English is the *lingua franca* of Europe. According to the European Commission, some 84 per cent of young people in the EC are currently learning English as a second language. No language – neither French in the Middle Ages, nor Latin before it – has ever been taught so widely in Europe.

It is *the* world language, the most popular second language in China and Japan and spoken by 760–800 million people around the world. Some 1.2 billion people live in countries where English is the official language.

This often has an adverse effect on native speakers. It makes them more reluctant to learn other languages (and the only way really to understand a culture is to speak its language). According to EC figures, Anglophone Ireland has the worst score for language learning in Europe.

This international language cannot accurately be called "English" at all. It ought, rather, to be called world English, international English or Anglo-American. The language is no longer the intellectual property of Britain.

One of its great advantages as a

world language is that there is no academy to decide what is and what is not "good English". English, like the Common Law, is what it has become – a less formal and a more flexible instrument than either French or German. And it is seen in rich and poor countries alike as the language of modern consumerism. It holds out the (probably illusory) promise of prosperity and material progress.

If international English has a spiritual home it is in the United States. Opposition to the spread of English is often animated by a certain anti-Americanism, or the kind of narrow-minded nationalism that is re-emerging in post-communist Europe.

But for most of those who learn it, it is a language of hope – "the true Esperanto" as George Steiner calls it. For young people in Europe there is no chauvinism involved in choosing it as a second language, nor does it follow that a student of English has an interest in British culture. This is not well understood in Britain. The language has become a sign of a cosmopolitan, outward-looking attitude to life, not of the insularity with which Britain is all too often associated.

European English is spoken

from Brussels to Bratislava and as a first or second language by more than half the people in the European Community. The percentage of young people learning English as a foreign language at school in the EC countries, apart from Britain and Ireland, is 100 per cent in Denmark, 95 per cent in the Netherlands, 91 per cent in Luxembourg, 90 per cent in France, 84 per cent in Germany, 80 per cent in Belgium, 76 per cent in Greece, 72 per cent in Italy, 65 per cent in Spain and 55 per cent in Portugal.

The EC is debating whether to recognise more languages, such as Welsh, Basque, Catalan or Frisian. Countries like Britain and France are opposing the idea because they say it will mean more bureaucracy.

But what could be more bureaucratic than the present system which equates European languages with their national boundaries? Language is perhaps the greatest barrier to trade and the Single Market. Promoting English within the EC Lingua programme or perhaps some new EC programme would surely be the cheapest, most sensible way of overcoming it.

Jon Packer

EXAM TIP

The multiple-matching exam question below is in two parts. Questions **1–4** ask you to decide how many people speak four different languages, by choosing from seven figures which all appear in the texts. Questions **5–8** ask you to complete four sentences by choosing from seven possible answers. Only one answer is correct for each item and no answer can be used more than once.

In the exam this type of question is usually quite straightforward and requires you to find information stated in the text. It is not necessary to read the whole text in detail but you should scan it for the appropriate passages and then read those in detail.

Occasionally, when the answer is not immediately obvious, you may have to infer the answer from the information given.

The extra options are designed to complicate the task and are very often *almost* right for a particular question. It is therefore a good idea to double-check when you eliminate an option.

2 ⌨ *Exam Question* Answer questions **1–8** by referring to the three newspaper articles about different languages.
For questions **1–4**, answer by matching the number of people **A–G** from Box 1 with the languages they speak. There are three extra figures.

Box 1
A 700,000
B 1.2 billion
C 800 million
D 200,000
E 15 million
F 300,000
G 2 million

1 Breton ☐
2 Frisian ☐
3 English is spoken regularly by ☐
4 Dutch ☐

Read Text 3 and complete sentences **5–8** with the endings **H–N** in Box 2. There are three extra sentence endings.

5 Ireland ☐
6 Portugal ☐
7 Denmark ☐
8 America ☐

Box 2
H is the spiritual home of 'world English'.
I has the worst foreign language learning record.
J has the best foreign language learning record.
K has the lowest proportion of young people learning English.
L has the highest proportion of young people learning English.
M is opposed to official recognition of minority languages.
N is in favour of promoting English alone within the EC Lingua programme.

3 🔊 What do the three extra figures in Box 1 refer to?

4 🔊 Which of the following categories of text type would you say the articles belong to?

a) informational
b) opinion
c) imaginative
d) descriptive

Which articles are the most/least objective?

5 🔊 What arguments does the writer of Text 3 put forward to support the use of English as an international communication medium?

6 Do you agree with the point of view expressed in Text 3?
Do you sympathise with the people fighting to save minority languages?
Do you think the issues raised in these articles are contradictory or is it possible to both promote the spread of English as a universal language of communication and save the minority regional languages?

Section B

1 🔊 Look at the title of the newspaper article in this section and decide which of the following the article is likely to be:

a) the expression of a writer's personal views
b) a news report on a specific event

Skim quickly through the article and see if you were right.

2 🔊 Decide whether the statements below are true or false in the context of the article.

1 In Britain it is bad manners to put your hands on the table when you are eating.
2 The Greeks are bad builders.
3 Americans only eat hamburgers and pizza.
4 The Finnish national dish is meat patties.
5 You have to tip Italian nurses.
6 The Spanish use kettles to heat their water.
7 In the USA you can have a snack at the chemist's.
8 The Turks celebrate name days.
9 Italian children receive their Christmas presents on Christmas eve.
10 The British go shopping on Sundays.

Is the information clearly stated or is it stated indirectly?

There'll always be nations

Katharine Whitehorn

I HAD a friend who never knew what to do with her hands at meals; brought up half in England – 'hands on your lap, dear' – and half in France – '*les mains sur la table*' – she was thoroughly confused.

Another couple I know built a little house in Greece, and joyfully completed it; the Greeks thought they were mad, because once the house is finished you have to pay tax on it – which is why so many Greek houses have iron rods sticking out of the top, to show there's more concrete to come. And a man who went to live in Turkey speaks feelingly of the unique piece of Turkish plumbing which combines a lavatory with a bidet-douche: 'If you don't know what that little handle is for, you rapidly learn how high you can jump from a sitting position.'

It is the small things which make the interesting differences between countries, and there are far more of them than ever appear at the level of diplomatic meetings and grand hotels. We think of ubiquitous pizzas and hamburgers, but forget the food you buy in the street – the chestnuts you get in London, tapas in Spain, lihapiirakka (meat patties) in Finland. Western medicine may be all of a piece – but how much plaster you get depends on where you are; right up the arm for a broken wrist in France, a whole-body plaster (or so I am told) for a little finger in Italy – and you'd better tip the nurses, too.

Cookers may be made anywhere, but the Dutch scarcely use their ovens, they prefer to wallow in margarine on top of the stove; the French don't expect a grill except inside the oven, and rarely seem to sell non-stick spatulas to go with their non-stick pans; the Spanish don't go in for kettles. I thought the Americans were just unbearably fussy, the way they obsessively rinse plates – until I realised that American dishwashers actually don't have filters. And there's a school of sociology which says you can determine a country's level of civilisation by the efficiency of its bottle tops: the more gashes on your hand, the more primitive the country you're trying to drink in.

Computers, compact discs, cameras may be the same everywhere – but we go to a chemist's to buy film, because the British used to get their developing fluid there; other nations don't. A continental chemist may austerely sell nothing but drugs, few will sell hair-slides and tights and hot water bottles like ours; and none of them sell two eggs over easy and a cup of cawfee, as in the States.

In some ways one wishes things were *more* standardised: if only all telephones made the same noises to tell you they're engaged or ringing or on the blink. Or if they put the lights and screen-wipers always on the same side of the steering-wheel, we'd flash our wipers in anger so much less often. And even if countries can't agree on how much summer time to have, could they not at least agree to change on the same day? As it is, airline schedules are total chaos for two weeks every autumn.

But times and festivals are among the hardest things to shift. It's no good telling a Turk to celebrate his birthday and not his name day, or trying to make an Italian child, all agog on Christmas eve, wait till Christmas day, like us – quite apart from EC directive number 4783/AB 7, which decrees there shall always be a bank holiday in any country where I happen to have run out of currency.

Or take Sundays. Our flat traditional Sunday of churchgoing and inertia has just about had it; the only pity is that they didn't legalise proper shopping before car-boot sales turned half the nation into fences for stolen goods. But do you remember when they spoke with horror of the wicked 'continental Sunday'? It conjured up visions of the bibulous French singing in the streets; plainly, no one cared even to think about a German Sunday, when you not only can't shop, you can't even wash your car lest the swooshing of your hose disturbs your neighbours.

It is the fear of losing these differences, I am sure, that makes people scared of getting close to Europe; my guess is that they will stay unchanged, like molluscs on the ocean floor beneath the tide of change. For it *is* a tide. Just as businesses go with a rhythmic predictability from centralisation to more on the spot autonomy back to centralisation again, so nations group together into larger units and then split up again, with local habits going on very much as before.

The big groups seem immortal – while they last. We take it for granted the USA is forever, but it's been all in one piece for less than a century; Bolivar's vision of a united South America didn't even last as long as his lifetime. No one would have guessed that the monolith of the USSR would break up so suddenly; yet when it did, there were Georgians who had gone right on speaking Georgian, Ukrainians with their national identity intact, Muslims who'd stuck to their customs throughout. What matters is not that the groupings and re-groupings happen; they always will; but whether people carve each other up in the process. The astonishing achievement of the EC is that they haven't.

The remarkable resilience of nationality, of tribal instincts and regional habits has always been the despair of reformers and tyrants alike, from Butcher Cumberland to Lenin to Saddam Hussein; I now see it as a saving grace. We British might or might not man the barricades for our defence policy or working hours or ramshackle legal system, but try and tamper with the pallid sanctity of our sausages and the spirit of Churchill and Drake awakes at once; which is how it should be.

3 🔑 *Exam Question* For questions **1–5**, complete sentences about national characteristics with one of the endings **A–H** in the box. There are three extra sentence endings. Try to take no more than five minutes to do this question.

1 The Dutch ☐	**A** have a very efficient medical system.
2 The French ☐	**B** do not celebrate birthdays.
3 Turks ☐	**C** like fried food.
4 The Greeks ☐	**D** live in single-storey, concrete houses.
5 Germans ☐	**E** are not very respectful of Sunday.
	F avoid paying property taxes.
	G grill everything they eat.
	H do very little on Sundays.

STUDY TIP

Some texts are heavily biased and present only the writer's views on a particular topic – texts written in the first person may often be of this type. Others are more objective, presenting facts and quoting or presenting other people's views. But hardly any texts are completely objective: a writer always reveals something about his or her views, either explicitly or by the way he or she chooses to write about a topic.

A writer may use phrases like: 'My guess is', 'What matters is', 'I now see it as', 'I believe', etc. In this case, interpreting the writer's opinions is straightforward. Alternatively, a writer may use a number of less obvious ways of expressing his or her views, such as:

– The choice of words, e.g. 'The *remarkable* resilience of nationality …'. In this sentence, the word 'remarkable' reveals the writer's view of national resilience.

– The way a writer chooses to describe or discuss something, e.g. the use of exaggeration or irony to attract the reader's attention or to mock.

4 ☛ **Read the article and decide which of the statements below the writer would agree with.**

1 Life would be easier and travelling more enjoyable if everything was standardised.
2 It is small differences between countries which are interesting.
3 National identity and habits are extremely difficult to change.
4 Local habits are unlikely to change very much with the creation of a unified Europe.
5 The USA will always be one united country.

5 ☛ **In the sentences below the writer expresses her personal opinions by her choice of words. Underline the words which reveal her opinion.**
Example: 'I thought the Americans were just unbearably fussy, the way they obsessively rinse plates.'
These words tell us that she does not approve of this American trait.

1 '... (the Dutch) prefer to wallow in margarine on top of the stove ...'
2 'A continental chemist may austerely sell nothing but drugs, ...'
3 'Our flat traditional Sunday of churchgoing and inertia has just about had it ...'
4 '... the only pity is that they didn't legalise proper shopping before car-boot sales turned half the nation into fences for stolen goods.'
5 '... a German Sunday, when you not only can't shop, you can't even wash your car lest the swooshing of your hose disturbs your neighbours.'

6 ☛ **The writer also expresses her opinions in a more direct way.**
Example: 'It is the small things which make the interesting differences between countries, and there are far more of them than ever appear at the level of diplomatic meetings and grand hotels.'
Find other examples of clearly stated opinions in the article.

11

The living world

> The aim of this unit is to focus on the following:
>
> - understanding the main ideas in a text
> - understanding the writer's attitude and purpose and tone of the text
> - inferring meaning from context and vocabulary
>
> The multiple-matching exam question requires you to complete sentences with phrases which express a relationship of cause and effect.

Section A

1 Are there wolves in your country? What sort of reputation do they have? Are there legends and folk tales about wolves? Write down eight or ten words which you associate with wolves.

2 ☞ The newspaper article in this section is about efforts to save the European wolf from extinction. Read the title of the article and the first and last paragraphs.
Which of these questions do you think the article is likely to answer?

1 Who were Romulus and Remus?
2 Why has the Italian wolf conservation programme been successful?
3 Why have wolves been hunted?
4 How many wolves are there in Europe?
5 What other famous legends are there about wolves?
6 What must be done to save the European wolf?

3 Look quickly through the article and underline the sentence or words that best sum up the main idea of each paragraph. Try not to take more than five minutes. Check whether the article answers the questions in 2.

Wolves are refusing to pack it in

Malcolm Smith

WOLVES are still found roaming wild only 20 kilometres or so from the Colosseum in Rome. They are among a few hundred descendants of the legendary she-wolf that suckled Romulus and Remus, the city's founders, to have survived into the 20th century.

Prospects that the Italian wolf, *canis lupus italicus*, will see in the next century are better now than at any time in the past 20 years. The number of wolves in Italy has increased from an all-time low of about 100 in the early Seventies to between 350 and 400 today.

However, the future for the wolf is bleak elsewhere in Europe. Wolves are left in only eight of its 23 member states. Western Europe has a total of a few thousand wolves, according to a recent report by the Council of Europe.

The wolf has had a bad press. Children's stories and folk tales have conditioned countless generations to fear and despise Europe's largest carnivore. Much of the hatred stems from the belief that they kill people as well as livestock.

But it is almost impossible to find authenticated cases of attacks on adult humans, except by rabid wolves. There are a few instances of small children being attacked while wandering alone in remote places.

Two children were killed in Galicia, in Spain, at the end of the 1960s; another two in 1974. On both occasions the attacks were made by a lone female wolf. But attacks like this are extremely rare. More people probably die on Europe's roads every day than have been killed by wolves over the past thousand years. Ironically, it is in northern countries like Norway and Sweden, generally considered as environmentally aware, that the wolf is on the verge of extinction.

Larger populations have managed to survive in southern Europe – and also notably in Turkey. There were once tens of thousands in Spain and Portugal, where perhaps only 1,700 now roam.

The decline of wolves in Italy until the 1970s appears to have been halted and their range has extended slightly over the past decade, giving rise to optimism among conservationists.

Because of long isolation, the wolves of Spain and Portugal, and of Italy, are genetically distinct from those in the rest of Western Europe, and from those in Eastern Europe and Asia, where wolves are more common.

Biologists regard them as different sub-species, and their feeding habits differ. Italian wolves have a varied diet of small rodents and hares, fruit, plants, food scraps and the occasional domestic animal. Spanish wolves take food scraps too, but prey mainly on small wild boar and game birds.

This isolation of many wolf populations heightens concern for their survival. Dr Hartmut Jungius, of the Worldwide Fund for Nature, says: "Wolves are an endangered species. They are a priority for conservation in south and west Europe, where their populations are isolated; less so in eastern Europe, where they are connected to the larger populations in Asia."

Italy's successful wolf protection programme, launched in 1987, has doubled the animals' numbers and the habitats available to them. Their range is also increasing, rapidly so in Tuscany and Liguria. The country's leading wolf expert, Dr Luigi Boitani, of Rome University, says that a small number are being bred in captivity so that reintroductions can be considered where they have been driven to extinction.

A major step forward has been the provision of compensation by several of Italy's regional governments for unfortunate farmers

---

4 🔊 Read the article and complete the chart.

Country	Wolves are legally protected Yes: ✓ No: ✗	Numbers are increasing: + declining: – stable: ----
Italy		
Finland		
Spain		
Portugal		
Greece		

whose livestock have fallen prey to wolves. Two or three hundred sheep can be killed in just a few hours. Feral dogs – domestic animals that have reverted to the wild – can do the same, and the carnage is all too often blamed on wolves.

Italy has about 80,000 feral dogs plus another 200,000 stray domestic dogs, vastly outnumbering wolves, says Dr Boitani. He is worried about the risk of these dogs interbreeding with wolves, wiping out the Italian wolf as we know it. Ironically, he says, though wolves are often reviled, animal protection organisations leap to the defence of stray and feral dogs. In Scandinavia the main conflict between wolf and man hinges on game animals, especially reindeer, because they are so important in the local economy.

In the north, east and extreme south of Finland, for instance, wolves can be legally hunted in winter. In central Finland they are protected, although the government can – and does – grant special licences to kill them. In the 1980s an average of 41 wolves were killed every year, despite full compensation for livestock losses. Wolves would never survive in Finland without the steady influx of animals from northern Russia, where they are more abundant.

In Greece the wolf has been legally protected since 1983 – in theory. But organised hunts and poisoning are commonplace, apparently sanctioned by the authorities.

While numbers seem to be falling in Portugal, in spite of legal protection since 1988, they have risen in Spain over the past ten years. An increase in habitat and food availability, and controls on hunting, seem to be the reasons.

The Council of Europe has proposed a 12-point plan to conserve Europe's wolves, including captive breeding programmes, controls on feral dogs, compensation for livestock losses – and better education to foster greater understanding of these impressive animals. It wants countries with wolves to set aside areas in which they are fully protected, but to allow limited control in other areas, if need be. Dr Boitani says each fully protected area should cover at least 20,000 square kilometres.

But the European wolf is far from safe, even in Italy. Its increasing population there remains scattered in fragmented areas along the Apennine mountains. Greater awareness of the issues involved in its conservation, better co-operation between countries with surviving populations, and learning from the success of the Italian programme could guarantee a better future for the legendary wolf.

5 ↷ *Exam Question*   Complete sentences **1–8** with one of the endings **A–K** in the box. There are three extra sentence endings.

1 Wolves are a priority for conservationists in southern and western Europe … ☐
2 Wolves are universally hated … ☐
3 Conservationists are less pessimistic today about the future of wolves in western Europe … ☐
4 Italian farmers accept more easily the presence of wolves today … ☐
5 Wolves are hunted in parts of Finland mainly … ☐
6 Wolves are still present in Finland … ☐
7 Spanish and Italian wolves are genetically distinct from their Scandinavian cousins … ☐
8 In Spain the number of wolves has risen in the last ten years … ☐

because
A traditional stories have created an irrational fear of them.
B they cross the border from Russia.
C compensation is paid when livestock are killed.
D they are not legally protected.
E they were reintroduced from Turkey.
F the wolf population has stabilised.
G of hunting restrictions and an increase in available food.
H their populations have long been isolated.
I governments do not pay farmers compensation.
J they compete with humans for game.
K their isolation makes them particularly vulnerable.

EXAM TIP

The multiple-matching exam question in this section asks you to match the two parts of a sentence using the word *because*. Any of the phrases **A–K** would form a grammatically correct sentence with any of the sentences **1–8**. However, only one combination is correct in the context of the passage.

This question is designed to test your ability to recognise relationships of cause and effect. These relationships are not always clearly stated but are sometimes only implied by the information that is given, in which case you may need to infer the missing information. This involves a close reading of parts of the text and a good understanding of the main ideas.

6 ◌─○ Where do the writer's sympathies lie? With the conservationists or with their opponents? Or is he indifferent?

7 ◌─○ Which of the following phrases best express the writer's purpose?

a) to support the conservationists' cause
b) to present objective information
c) to present both sides of a controversial issue
d) to persuade the reader that wolves are harmless

8 What are your views on the controversial issue of protecting and reintroducing wolves?
What arguments is an anti-conservationist likely to develop?
Write a short letter to the newspaper in which the article appeared expressing your anger and opposition to the protection of wolves.

Section B

1 ◌─○ Read the title and opening paragraphs of the article below and answer the questions as you go along.

Are animals as dumb as they look?

Bees communicate by dancing, and plovers will fake a broken wing to foil a predator, but do they know what they're doing?
Stuart Sutherland reports

When I was studying the behaviour of octopuses, there was one beast that particularly intrigued me. As I approached its tank, it would swim towards the surface.

1 What do we learn about the writer?

Having anchored itself to the side of the tank and filled its mantle with water, it would raise its siphon above the surface and blast a strong jet of sea water into my face. It would then retreat to the bottom of its tank, where it would roll about shaking with laughter – or so it seemed to me.

2 Why is the last phrase important for the overall meaning of the paragraph?

> I tell this story because almost the only human capacity for which Donald Griffin, the discoverer of echo location in bats, can find no analogue among animals is a sense of humour.

3 What do we learn about Donald Griffin?

4 The writer deliberately includes the anecdote about the octopus as an introduction to Griffin's work. What does this suggest about his attitude to this work?

2 ⌁ Look quickly through the rest of the article on page 84 and decide whether your prediction about the writer's attitude is confirmed.

3 ⌁ The writer lists a number of 'complex and seemingly intelligent activities of animals'. Scan the text and write down what these activities are. What example(s) does he mention for each activity?
Example: *Animals deceive*   e.g. plovers and chimpanzees

STUDY TIP

Every writer assumes that he or she shares a certain amount of knowledge with the reader. But this is not always the case. You may only become aware of this underlying assumption when faced with something you do not understand because you do not share the writer's knowledge.

It is useful to be aware of this type of comprehension problem because even if you do not share the writer's knowledge, you can very often infer what it is by reading the text carefully. However, you must bear in mind that not all assumed knowledge can be inferred from the context and that, in practice, this is rarely a major problem.

The writer of the article here discusses the activities of bees, beavers and chimpanzees without telling the reader what these animals are. He assumes, probably correctly, that the reader will know this.

4 ⌁ Answer the following questions and decide whether the text provides clues to meaning.

1 What is echo location in bats?
2 What is a plover?
3 What is the Egyptian vulture? Why does it crack ostrich eggs?
4 Who is Helen Keller? Why is she mentioned?
5 What does *sine qua non* mean?
6 What is American Sign Language likely to be?

Is it possible to guess the meaning from the context? Underline the words and phrases which help you guess the meaning.
Which questions above are impossible to answer with the information provided? Is this a problem for understanding the rest of the passage?

In *Animal Minds* (University of Chicago Press), a delightful book, he recounts some of the more complex and seemingly intelligent activities of animals. They often deceive, he believes, deliberately. For example, the plover on spotting a potential predator flies haltingly away from its nest, feigning a broken wing. The predator, always eager for wounded and hence easy prey, follows and is led away from the eggs or young.

And there was that wily old chimpanzee (not recorded by Griffin), who having picked some especially succulent bananas, found himself surrounded by other members of his species begging to have some: he grunted and pointed as much as to say "that way", but indicated the opposite direction to the banana tree.

The use of tools is widespread in the animal kingdom. Chimpanzees fish for termites with sticks they have shaped in a suitable way, while the Egyptian vulture drops stones on ostrich eggs that are too tough to crack with its beak.

Even agriculture is quite widely practised. For example, some ants construct special chambers containing fungus and then bring leaves to nourish it. The leaves can be a metre in diameter requiring several ants to haul them in. The ants have even discovered the value of manure, for which they use their own faeces. As for engineering, beavers are adept at making dams. When there is a frost and the water freezes they cut holes towards the top of the dam to create an air space below the ice through which they can breathe.

The observations and anecdotes that Griffin reports are intended not merely to interest and amuse, but to demonstrate that animals are conscious. He is anxious to prove they have language, though this is not a *sine qua non* of consciousness, since Helen Keller reports that she was conscious before she had learned a language.

It is, of course, true that many animals communicate. Bees convey information to one another about flowers containing nectar, by a complex dance performed on a vertical surface. The angle to the vertical of their movements indicates the direction of the flowers with respect to the sun, while the movements' lengths signal the distance of the flowers and their vigour denotes the quality of the nectar. Bees also dance to signal the location of the new hive.

Curiously, although their dances are limited to one or two themes (admittedly important ones if you happen to be a bee), they are perhaps the most complex form of "language" known in animals. The bees' dance is almost certainly innate, as are so many other complex activities of insects. As Griffin points out, that does not mean it is performed unconsciously. However, it does suggest that it is not done deliberately, a question he does not discuss.

In recent years much effort has been devoted to training chimpanzees to communicate using American Sign Language. They can learn individual gestures signifying their wants or even naming objects,

but they fail to put them together to communicate new meanings in the way that human infants do.

The "language" they have learned is so impoverished that it bears almost no relationship to human speech. Dolphins appear to have a rich system of communication, but it has not yet been deciphered.

Having established that bees do it, educated chimpanzees do it, Griffin goes on to claim that if a species exhibits seemingly intelligent and purposeful behaviour, then it must be conscious, but he does not adequately discuss the grounds on which we ascribe consciousness to others. We do so solely because we know that we ourselves are conscious and by analogy we conclude that any beings sufficiently like ourselves must also be conscious.

The relevant aspects of similarity include not merely behaviour but the organisation of the brain. Because chimpanzees are so like people, few would want to deny them consciousness – they have 97 per cent of their genes in common with us. Most people would also agree that dogs and cats, and possibly rats and mice are conscious.

But the nervous system of insects is so different from ours, and their capacity for learning so small, that if they have consciousness at all it must be in an attenuated form. The interesting question is not whether animals have consciousness, but what benefits it brings to those, including ourselves, that do.

5 🔑 Decide who would agree with the following statements: the writer, Griffin or both.

1 Animals are conscious of their actions.
2 Animals do not necessarily do things consciously.
3 It is not necessary to have language in order to be conscious.
4 An innate activity is not necessarily an activity performed unconsciously.
5 An activity performed instinctively is not done deliberately.
6 When animals do things which have a purpose, they must be conscious of what they are doing.
7 It cannot be assumed that animals are conscious of their actions just because humans are.

6 🔑 Which of the following describes the writer's attitude to Griffin's work?

impressed   critical   complementary   condemning
non-committal

7 In the last sentence of the article the writer asks a question which he feels is important. Rewrite the question in a more straightforward manner. Write two or three sentences in answer to the question.

12 Communications

The aim of this unit is to focus on the following:

– identifying the purpose of a paragraph or a whole text

– inferring and understanding the writer's intentions and attitude

– dealing with difficult vocabulary

The multiple-choice exam question focuses on the writer's purpose, the tone of the text and the aim of the text as a whole.

Section A

1 Do you use any of the following machines?

> camcorder   home computer   portable computer
> microwave oven   mobile telephone   car phone
> telephone answering machine   fax   video recorder

Which would you most like to own?
Which would you have little use for?

2 ☎ The article on page 88 is about fax machines. Read the first paragraph of the article and decide which statement best summarises the main idea of the paragraph.

a) I have a fax so I must be an important and busy person.
b) I am an important and busy person so I have a fax.

Do you think the writer is serious when she describes herself as important and busy?

3 ☎ Find these phrases in the article and match them with their definitions. The same definition may be used more than once.

1 'the medium'	A the fax machine
2 'similarly technologically endowed'	B the message sent on a fax
3 'this exclusive club'	C communication by fax
4 'a bleeping machine'	D people without fax machines
5 'electronic postcards'	E people who own fax machines
6 'your masterpieces'	
7 'magic machines'	
8 'the great faxless underclass'	

EXAM TIP

One of the questions in a series of multiple-choice questions may ask you to decide what the purpose of a particular part of a passage is. For this type of question it may be useful to ask yourself these questions:

— Why has the writer written it?
— What effect does it have on the whole passage?

This type of question tests your ability to infer information which is not stated clearly so you will usually need to read the whole text carefully before deciding.

You may also be asked about the purpose or aim of the whole text. In this case the question is likely to come at the end of the series of multiple-choice questions.

You may find it helpful to ask yourself these questions:

— Does the text present the writer's own views?
— Is it mainly informational, presenting facts and figures?
— Is it persuasive? as in an advertisement
— Is it critical? as in a film or book review
— Is it amusing? etc.

4 ☛ **Find the following statements in the article.**

1 'the index of my success is my faxability'
2 'I fax therefore I am.'
3 'the medium has more cachet than the message'
4 'knowledge is power'
5 'the great faxless underclass'
6 'speed feeds our sense of self-importance'
7 'It's not what you say but how fast you say it.'
8 'Faxes are about declarations rather than dialogue.'

Now match the statements 1–8 with their explanations.

a) The way you communicate is more important than what you communicate.
b) Being able to communicate a message quickly is more important than the message itself.
c) People who do not own fax machines are inferior beings.
d) The fax is not so much a means of communication as a means for the owner to assert his or her self-importance.
e) To own a fax machine is proof that a person is successful.
f) Doing things quickly makes you feel important.
g) You are aware that the fax is not essential, but to maintain the illusion of your superiority you must not admit it.
h) The fax is a declaration of your existence among the people who count.

Fax and faxability

Suzanne Moore

I am extremely important. So important that all kinds of people might need to communicate with me 24 hours a day. Mere phone calls are not good enough, letters take days, or at least a day, and meeting face to face – well, obviously that is out of the question. No, the index of my success is my faxability. God only knows what international incidents have been averted by my matt black fax machine. For I am now at the centre of a vast global communications network, all of which is instantly faxable, and made up of busy, busy people who cannot possibly wait for that vital document a minute longer.

"Fax it to me," we say snappily, presuming that we are in the company of the similarly technologically endowed. "What do you mean you haven't got one?" we gasp in amazement at their willingness to admit they are not a member of this exclusive club. After all, membership only sets you back £400 or so and for this you get to recite daily our motto: "I fax therefore I am." Once you are in possession of one of those magic machines a new world opens up to you. A world of escalating urgency, a world where the most mundane information becomes somehow more significant because it arrives via a bleeping machine, a world where the medium has more cachet than the message.

The fax machine, like the camcorder, has come into its own in the Nineties. The affordability of this technology has meant that the democracy of instantaneous communication has filtered down to us all. So now we are all dutifully engaged in this orgy of electronic impulses, recording and erasing, faxing and receiving. But what are we actually communicating apart from the fact that we are *in communication*? The urgent messages we send each other on these electronic postcards are often little more than reminders that, "Yes, we have the technology, even if we have little use for it."

Yet because we know that knowledge is power we

cannot admit as much, for to do so would be to join the great faxless underclass. Instead we pretend that every doodle, every hurried sentence is somehow so earth-shatteringly crucial that it must immediately be signalled halfway round the world. For some like Philippe Starck, who designs by fax, this may be the case. But what do most of us use faxes for? We can now fax a pizza or a sandwich; we can fax afternoon radio shows with our funny stories; we can fax our bank manager; we can fax our resignation notice and nowadays we can even be fired by fax.

Although there is some argument about the legal status of any fax that purports to be contractual, the great benefit of all this is that it is done in public. Indeed what the latest batch of communications technology, from mobile phones to camcorders to faxes, have in common is that they no longer respect the old boundaries between public and private, work and leisure. If you fall down and break your leg, some idiot with a camcorder will be recording your pain and sending it to an amateur video show on TV. If someone sends you a humiliating rejection by fax, you can guarantee that everyone else will have read it before you.

Likewise, encouraged by insane advertising which advises us to turn our homes into extensions of our offices, there is now no time in which work cannot intrude on leisure. The answering and fax machines must always be switched on in case we miss some vital piece of information. But what exactly is it that for most of us cannot wait until tomorrow? We are not running countries, or multinational corporations, but the trick is to act like we are. In our "accelerated culture" speed feeds our sense of self-importance. It's not what you say but how fast you say it, and a fax provides instant gratification that this is the case. Faxes are about declarations rather than dialogue.

But even this delicious frenzy of non-communication can go wrong. Fax terrorists sabotage business by bunging up the machine with 50 pages saying nothing but "Peace and love". And who has had a fax gone astray? As you slot your paper into the hungry mouth how do you really know where it is going, that you have the right number, that you are not sending your masterpieces into oblivion? Worse still: they can break down.

Since my two-year-old poured a can of coke into mine I have not received any faxes at all. The sad truth is that I never did get many. Apart from the odd work stuff they would mostly be from friends trying out their new fax machines. Having received theirs, I could then fax them back to tell them that they were in full working order. See, I told you I was important.

5 🔊 *Exam Question*   Answer questions **1–6** by choosing **A**, **B**, **C** or **D**. Try to do this question in no more than 15 minutes.

1 The purpose of the first paragraph is to
   A interest and surprise the reader.
   B explain why the writer needs a fax.
   C convince the reader of the importance of faxes.
   D focus on the legitimate uses for faxes.

2 Why do a large number of people own fax machines today?
   A because the fax is a symbol of success
   B because it is the fastest way of sending a document
   C because it is more reliable than sending a letter
   D because it is still too expensive for most people

3 The writer thinks that most people use the fax
   A to order pizzas and sandwiches.
   B to send vital documents.
   C to give themselves a sense of self-importance.
   D to help them become successful.

⫸➔

4 The general tone of the text is
   A serious.
   B ironic.
   C passionate.
   D matter-of-fact.

5 The writer uses exaggeration in order to
   A demonstrate how ridiculous it is for most people to have a fax.
   B prove to the reader that faxes can be sabotaged and break down.
   C show why her friends are getting fax machines.
   D describe the importance of speedy communications in the modern business world.

6 What is the writer's main aim in this article?
   A to express her views on fax machines and modern communications
   B to persuade the reader to buy a fax
   C to inform the reader of the advantages and disadvantages of faxes
   D to justify the writer's ownership of a fax

6 ☛ Find the following phrases in the text. What effect do they have on the tone of the article?

'I am extremely important.'
'Mere phone calls'
'busy, busy people'

Can you find any other phrases which have a similar effect?

7 Did you enjoy reading the article? Would you say it is effective? Do you agree with the writer?

8 Can you think of another way of writing about the same subject? Write an alternative first paragraph of an article which conveys the same general ideas but presents them differently. Think about the tone of the article.

Section B

1 How do you like to communicate with people?

by phone   by letter or fax   in person

What are the advantages and disadvantages of each means of communicating?

2 ☞ The texts in this section are about using the Internet, which is a world-wide system of communicating with people using computers and telephone lines. The following information about the Internet is all true. First, read it so that you know a little more about the Internet.

a) You can have written conversations with people around the world using the Internet for the price of a local telephone call.
b) You need special equipment called a modem to add to your computer in order to use it for world-wide communications.
c) You need to subscribe to an on-line service in order to use your phone line to exchange messages around the world.
d) There are many forums around the world which cater for your own special interests, where you can read or leave messages.
e) You need to use certain typographical conventions in written messages to show emotions and meanings which would be obvious if you were speaking face to face with people.

Now read the two texts and choose the information which best summarises their content.

3 ☞ Who are the texts written for?

a) people who have used the Internet a great deal
b) people who are starting to use the Internet
c) people who have never used or even heard of the Internet

4 ☞ The following sentences all belong to the first text. Decide where they should go.

a) You are allowed to tell other readers about something they may be interested in, but you must not promote your own product.
b) But there are specialist conferences, scheduled for particular times.
c) This rule book is authoritative; extraordinarily so given that nobody owns, or polices, the Internet.
d) Each special-interest group will have an easily accessible section labelled FAQ, for Frequently Asked Questions.
e) This is the computer equivalent of Citizen's Band (CB) radio.

5 ☞ Which piece of information do both texts refer to?

THE IDIOT'S GUIDE TO CYBERSPACE

Netiquette

Now that you are ready to join an electronic street-corner discussion about a subject that interests you – anything from Venezuelan culture to a Volkswagen's mechanics – you will need to learn the language of cyberspace.

To start with you will simply want to see what special-interest groups, or forums, are around without actually contributing anything. You do this by clicking on the "browse" or "preview" icon displayed on your screen. At some stage, though, you will want to join in. Perhaps you want to know who the next Venezuelan finance minister is likely to be, or where you can get go-faster stripes for your Beetle. When you click out of "browse", a menu will appear asking whether you want to join the group: click on the "yes" icon, or type "yes" and you can join in.

Before you utter a single (written) word, however, it is essential to learn your Netiquette. **1** … If you transgress, you are likely to be "flamed" or assaulted by abusive messages from outraged users.

Rule one. Make sure you are not asking a question that has been asked a zillion times before. **2** …

Rule two. Do not advertise. **3** …

Rule three. Do not flood several groups with the same message; this is called "spamming" after the Monty Python spam sketch.

Rule four. Do not use capital letters: this is the computer equivalent of shouting.

There are ways, however, of expressing mood in messages. The written word can be cold and flat compared with voice and body language: jokes can be misinterpreted or missed altogether, as can irony and scepticism. The on-line world has developed its own symbols (called "emoticons") and acronyms to make sure tone is understood.

The most widely used is :-). Turn the page on the side and you should see a smile. Other common ones are :-((frowning), :-> (biting sarcasm), ;-) (winky smile). Less common ones are :*) (user is drunk), :'(((user is crying), :-& (user is tongue-tied).

Acronyms are also used to save time and space: TTBOMK (to the best of my knowledge), ROFL (rolling on floor laughing), TANJ (there ain't no justice). And plenty more.

Once you have your Netiquette cracked, you may feel brave enough to take part in a "real time" – that is, live – chat or conference. **4** … Several enthusiasts at a time can join in jargon-ridden conversations on esoteric and often dull subjects. On-line services have their own chat areas: on some, anyone can take part, for others you have to ask permission.

Most of the conversation is general and banal. **5** … If Italian cookery or Sci Fi is your interest, you can join in a more useful "discussion" with other well-informed parties: these are advertised in the relevant special-interest group.

David Bowen

STUDY TIP

You may often be confronted with unusual language, such as jargon. Jargon consists of words or expressions which are used by a fairly restricted number of users in connection with a professional or personal interest. This sort of language is not very common in everyday use. You may also find examples of culture-specific language, the meaning of which is only clear to someone from inside the culture. It is surprising, nevertheless, how even complex passages often contain clues which will allow you to guess the general meaning of jargon and culture-specific language.

Sometimes the words and expressions are explained, with an explanation or synonym in brackets or followed by "…, or …" and "…, *that is*, …".

Sometimes it is clear that the writer is using jargon because the word or expression is placed in inverted commas, e.g. "… *you are likely to be 'flamed' or assaulted* …".

It's useful to learn these typographical conventions which may help you deal with unusual language.

Understanding forum conventions

When you post written messages, the normal body language and expressions that accompany speech are absent. A wry comment is usually accompanied by a slight smile. But how can you smile in writing? Without the smile, your comment may be misinterpreted as sarcasm.

One of the most typical mistakes that newcomers make is the use of capital letters. On the Internet, these are the equivalent of raising your voice. In fact, many frequent users complain that a message using capital letters actually "sounds" like shouting. Consider the following three versions of the same sentence, for example:

Let me tell you what I really think.

Let me tell you what I REALLY think.

LET ME TELL YOU WHAT I REALLY THINK.

As you read these, you may notice that the *really* in the second sentence gives the impression that the speaker's voice is being raised. This version is the equivalent of verbally saying, "Listen you, let me tell you what I REALLY think" – something you might want to do only if you are really steamed. The third sentence, which is unacceptable on the forums, comes across as if the speaker were shouting in a small room. Although writing in full capitalization is not against the rules, it is likely to cause comments from other users asking you to stop shouting.

A more acceptable way to emphasize a word or idea is to use an asterisk (*) or to indicate underlining with an underscore mark (_) before and after the word, as in the following examples:

Let me tell you what I *really* think.

Let me tell you what I _really_ think.

These softer versions emphasize that the comments are your true opinion but do not give the reader the impression that you are angry. Because the written word can be easily misinterpreted in the absence of facial expressions, gestures, and tone of voice, you should stick to the less strident versions.

Mark K. Bilbo

6 Decide if the following statements about the second text are true or false. Correct them where necessary.

1 You can't convey the same amount of meaning in writing as you can in speech.
2 Internet users are not allowed to use capital letters.
3 You use asterisks and dashes to show that you're only joking.
4 We communicate with facial expressions, gestures and tone of voice as well as words.

7 Are there any clues *within* the texts about the meaning of these unusual words and expressions?

cyberspace	Netiquette Beetle	forum	flamed
spamming	Monty Python spam sketch		emoticons
TTBOMK	CB		

8 Can you think of other conventions concerning the means of communication in 1? Think about starting and finishing the communication, gestures and body language.

9 Have you used the Internet? Do you think you would enjoy using it?

13

Science fiction?

The aim of this unit is to focus on the following:

- forming an overall impression and identifying the text type
- skimming for the main ideas and identifying arguments for and against
- evaluating a text and interpreting the writer's opinions

The 'gapped text' exam question requires you to reconstruct a text by inserting the missing paragraphs.

Section A

1 This section is about the development of robots, and in particular, the domestic robot. Make a list of the domestic jobs you do at home and order them according to how much you dislike doing them. Which jobs would you most like a robot to do in your home? Which jobs do you think will be done by robots in the future?

MAN MAID

The domestic help of the future is more likely to come equipped with oil, a manual and spare parts than a bucket and mop

NICK NUTTALL

i) At Danbury hospital in Connecticut, staff have been working with a new, enthusiastic recruit who trundles around wards, serving meals and bringing sterilised equipment to nurses at night.

2

ii) <u>This</u> is because Helpmate is a robot, and one of the first to make its way from the factory into service. Sue Taub, the manager of the dietary services division at Danbury hospital, says the robots have been used for about two years. There are plans to extend their roles into other areas, such as medical records, distribution and mail.

2

iii) The arrival of Helpmate highlights how some engineers are starting to fuse sensors, pneumatics, microchips, vision systems and other contemporary technologies to develop semi-intelligent machines which are a step closer to the science-fiction creatures of Isaac Asimov and other futuristic writers.

3

iv) <u>Now</u> a small but enthusiastic breed of mainly commercial engineers believe they have tackled a series of design problems which have held back "service" robots. At Portech – a company based within the University of Portsmouth and headed by Professor Arthur Collie – a climbing robot has been developed which can scale walls without the aid of any external ropes or frames.

4

v) <u>Meanwhile</u>, Armstrong Projects of Beaconsfield expects to have a prototype keyhole-surgery robot ready for tests at the end of the year. It is being developed to beam back images from inside the body, via a tube, so that a surgeon can see organs, and tumours, in areas ranging from the brain to the gall bladder.

5

vi) Other robots have or are being designed to do everything from milking cows and laying bricks to doing portraits. The worlds in which they work and move have a measure of predictability that is crucial for the technology to function safely and reliably.

6	

vii) Its computer brain is programmed with a detailed layout of wards, doors, corridors and nurses' stations so it does not get lost. Staff programme a task and location into Helpmate, using a cash-point style consul. The robot works out its location by calculating how far it has travelled through the building, using a system known as dead reckoning.

7	

viii) SCIENCE FICTION? Well, maybe. Several disastrous attempts have been made to produce a mechanised domestic servant – many of which have been thinly veiled attempts to cash in on robotic films, such as Star Wars. Nevertheless, Engelburger, past president of the Robot Institute of America, argues that, thoughtfully applied, some tasks could soon fall to a domestic machine. TRC has recently completed an evaluation of a robot able to perform a variety of jobs, which include pouring drinks, washing the car, preparing pre-packed food, cleaning the toilet and vacuuming the floor.

8	

ix) Whether humans will ever achieve the goal of developing a machine in their own image is doubtful, although Collie believes engineers are crossing a new threshold with the arrival of artificial computer intelligence and the emergence of new materials which are soft and flexible and can mimic muscle and skin. "We are coming out of an age in which machines are rigid structures into one where they are flexible and mobile. It is my view that intelligence in the living world came with movement," says Collie. "We are only at the stage where we can make something about as intelligent as an earthworm," he says. "Where this will end can hardly be envisaged."

A Special software is being designed for its computer brain so that the best route into a sensitive area, for example near the optic nerve, is offered to the surgeon. The robot designed by a team led by Dr Patrick Findlay, has a drill which should be accurate to within a millimetre.

B A few years ago, many researchers were sceptical that robots, in the foreseeable future, would accomplish anything more impressive than bashing metal, welding parts or spray-painting cars.

C The latest version of the machine, called Robug III, which is to receive development funding from the European Commission, will become a key aid in the inspection of nuclear power stations.

D Some researchers are now taking the technology of Helpmate and developing it to make a domestic machine, able to perform a variety of tasks, which include laying the table, serving cocktails and polishing the family silver.

E The robots, two of which operate at the hospital, can be instructed to carry out tasks in a matter of minutes by pressing a few buttons on their "bodies". They are costing the hospital half the hourly rate of a human while freeing staff to do more important tasks. They can even use lifts to make trips between floors.

F Helpmate, for example, merges vision, infra-red and ultrasound sensing systems to enable the machine to travel along corridors without banging into walls or objects. If a wheelchair suddenly moves into view, the machine will sense it and stop. It does not actually "see" the chair or person, but detects a fast shift in light which indicates danger ahead. The robot – developed by Transitions Research Corporation (TRC), a Danbury company founded by Joseph Engelberger – summons lifts and chooses floors, using a radio link.

G Stairs might prove too challenging for most robots. However, she argues that demographics are moving in the household robot's favour, as increasing numbers of elderly people choose to live in single-storey buildings.

H The employee is something of an administrator's dream. Unlike other nursing assistants, the new worker can toil up to 24 hours a day without needing a nap, does not idle at the coffee machine or gossip on the wards.

I The robot would have two arms, with as many as seven electro-mechanical joints and a detachable wrist. On to this, the robot could fit and remove a variety of attachments from its toolbox, including bath cleaners, toilet brushes and attachments for picking up plates and cutlery, and putting them into the dishwater.

2 🔊 Read the incomplete article and the paragraphs (A–I). Under which of these headings would you expect to find the article?

Health & science   Books   Science & technology   Industry
Food & health   Business   Economy

3 🔊 Which of these words would you use to describe the article?

informational   opinion   imaginative   descriptive

4 🔊 Group the paragraphs i–ix of the article under the headings below. Underline the words and expressions which helped you to decide.

Hospital robot   Robot technology · Surgeon's robot
Domestic robot   Climbing & service robots

5 🔊 Read the paragraphs A–I and group them under the headings in 4. Underline the words and expressions which helped you make your choice.

EXAM TIP

Remember, you may find the following steps helpful when doing the exam question below:

- Read the gapped text and paragraphs to form an overall impression of the text.
- Read the text again, underlining words and expressions which express the main ideas.
- Read the paragraphs and group together possible options according to the main ideas they express.
- Make a final choice by looking for linking clues: reference words, discourse markers, time adverbs.
- Check your answers by looking through the completed text – make sure the ideas are presented logically.

6 🔊 *Exam Question*   Match the paragraphs **A–I** with the gaps numbered **1–8**. There is one extra paragraph which does not belong in any of the gaps. Try to do this question in no more than ten minutes.

7 🔊 Some words and expressions have been underlined in the passage and paragraphs. Decide how they help link the passage together.
Example: <u>This</u> refers to the comment in the preceding paragraph: 'The employee is something of an administrator's dream.' It introduces an explanation.

8 If you had the choice between a robot and a human domestic help, which would you prefer?

Section B

1 The article in this section is about genetically engineered food. This is food which has been created by introducing genes into a species of plant or animal from another species.

Why do you think scientists are developing this technology?

Would you be prepared to buy this type of food?

Look at the list of people below. Who do you think is likely to approve of and who is likely to disapprove of this type of food?

| scientists | chefs | environmentalists | animal welfare groups |
| farmers | gourmets | consumers | |

STUDY TIP

In a text which discusses a controversial issue, the writer can present the different views for or against in a number of ways:

- by quoting what various people have written or said on the subject
- by summarising people's views
- by mentioning a number of arguments without specifying who supports them in particular (in this case words like *critics, sceptics, opponents, supporters, enthusiasts,* etc. are frequently used)
- by expressing his or her own views

---

2 ☞ Which of the statements below express arguments for genetic engineering and which against?

Who, from the list in 1, is likely to agree with these statements?

1 Genetic engineering may interfere with the balance of nature.
2 The development of new breeds of animals may lead to physical suffering.
3 There are no reliable controls for this technology.
4 Genetic engineering can create a wider variety of food sources.
5 Genetic research has led to a better understanding of living organisms.
6 The consequences of this technology are unknown.

3 According to the article, genetic engineering has already been used to modify the following foods:

mushrooms   tomatoes   grapefruit   potatoes

Look quickly through the article and find the sections which mention these vegetables. What modifications have been made to each vegetable and what are the advantages expected to be? Try to do this activity in no more than two minutes.

Monster vegetables escape from the lab

Genetically engineered food will soon be on the supermarket shelves

Keri Goldenhar

SUPERMARKET shoppers have never been more spoilt for choice. But just when we thought traditional systems of selective farming had created the most tempting array of foods money could buy, we are now being presented with the prospect of genetically created strains of cabbage, onion, tomato, potato and apple.

It may not tickle the fancy of food purists but it fires the imagination of scientists. Last week they discovered that the classic Parisian mushroom contains just the properties that, when genetically mixed with a wild strain of mushroom from the Sonora desert in California, could help it grow *en masse* while at the same time providing it with the resilience of the wild strain. "We have found a way of increasing the success rate from one to 90 per cent."

This is just one of the many products that, according to sceptics, are creating a new generation of "Frankenfoods". The first such food that may be consumed on a wide scale is a tomato which has been genetically manipulated so that it does not soften as it ripens. Critics say that the new tomato – which cost $25 million to research – is designed to stay on supermarket shelves for longer. It has a ten-day life span.

Not surprisingly, the ever-hungry US is leading the search for these forbidden fruit. By rearranging the genes of a grapefruit, a grower from Texas has created a sweet, red, thin-skinned grapefruit expected to sell at a premium over its California and Florida competitors.

For chip fanatics who want to watch their waistlines, new high-starch, low-moisture potatoes that absorb less fat when fried have been created, thanks to a gene from intestinal bacteria.

The scientists behind such new food argue that genetic engineering is simply an extension of animal and plant breeding methods and that by broad-

---

4 🔊 Decide where the following sentences should go in the article.

1 Western farmers have already bred cattle with more muscle than a skeleton can carry.
2 Supporters say the tomato, unappetisingly called Flavr Savr, will taste better because it will be able to mature on the branch longer.
3 Consumer opposition means that there are no genetically manipulated foods on the German market, and the Norwegian government has recently put research into genetically engineered foods on hold.
4 For example, if a corn gene is introduced into a wheat gene for pest resistance, will those who are allergic to corn then be allergic to wheat?
5 'Mushrooms in the past were almost impossible to cross,' says Philippe Callac, one of the three scientists working on the mushroom.

ening the scope of the genetic changes that can be made, sources of food are increased. Accordingly, they argue, this does not inherently lead to foods that are less safe than those developed by conventional techniques. But if desirable genes are swapped irrespective of species barriers, could things spiral out of control? "Knowledge is not toxic," said Mark Cantley, head of the biotechnology unit at the Organisation for Economic Co-operation and Development. "It has given us a far greater understanding of how living systems work at a molecular level and there is no reason for people to think that scientists and farmers should use that knowledge to do risky things."

Clearly, financial incentive lies behind the development of these bigger, more productive foods. But we may have only ourselves to blame. In the early days of mass food commerce, food varieties were developed by traditional methods of selective breeding to suit the local palate. But as suppliers started to select and preserve plant variants that had larger fruit, consumer expectations rose, leading to the development of the desirable clones. Still, traditionalists and gourmets in Europe are fighting their development.

Even in the pre-packaged US, where the slow-softening tomato will soon be reaching supermarkets, 1,500 American chefs have lent their support to the Pure Food Campaign which calls for the international boycott of genetically engineered foods until more is known about the consequences of the technology and reliable controls have been introduced.

In the short term, much of the technology remains untested and in the long term the consequences for human biology are unknown. Questions have arisen over whether new proteins in genetically modified foods could cause allergies in some people.

Then there are the vegetarians who may be consuming animal non-vegetable proteins in what they think is a common tomato, or the practising Jew who unknowingly consumes a fruit that has been enhanced with a pig's gene. As yet, producers are under no obligation to label "transgenic" products.

Environmentalists worry that new, genetically engineered plants may damage the natural environment. A genetically engineered pest-resistant strain of plant that comes into contact with a native strain, for example, could turn them into virulent weeds beyond chemical control.

Animal welfare groups worry about the quality of life of farm animals manipulated so that they produce more meat, milk and eggs but which may suffer physical damage in the process.

---

5 ☞ **What evidence is there in the article for the following statements?**

1 Genetically manipulated tomatoes taste better because they mature on the plant.
2 Genetic engineering does not lead to foods that are unsafe.
3 Gene swapping between species may damage the environment.
4 Many farmers are prepared to do risky things to increase their profits.
5 Financial gain is the primary factor in the development of genetic engineering.
6 The dangers of the technology are unknown because there are no controls.
7 It is likely to have serious long-term consequences on human biology.
8 Genetically engineered plants become uncontrollable weeds.

Which of the statements do you agree with?

6 🔑 The final paragraph of the article is missing. Look at two possible final paragraphs in which the writer expresses personal views on the development of genetic engineering. In which of the paragraphs does the writer do the following?

a) express unconditional approval of the development of genetic engineering
b) say that people's fears should not be dismissed
c) suggest that most fears are unfounded
d) state that this biotechnology may be more of a danger than a benefit
e) suggest that research should continue but be controlled

A Although genetic engineering is still in its infancy, many people are legitimately worried about the long-term consequences. It would certainly be a pity to deprive humanity of ways of solving serious medical and agricultural problems. But it would be an even greater pity if new, and as yet unknown problems, were created by the widespread use of this untested biotechnology.

B Many of these fears spring from ignorance. And although it is hard to separate the paranoia from the benefits, the fact remains that genetic engineering offers ways of solving serious medical and agricultural problems. It would be a huge loss if exaggerated fears prevented its potential from being explored.

Which would you say is the original final paragraph?

STUDY TIP

When evaluating the overall objectivity of a passage you may like to think about the following questions:

– How many different opinions are presented?
– Are the opinions of the different sides equally presented or is there an obvious bias?
– Does the writer express personal views at length?
– Are any important issues omitted?

7 Would you say the writer of this article has done the following?

– presented many of the arguments for and against genetic engineering very fairly
– shown prejudice in favour of the new technology
– used the article to promote personal views
– succeeded in informing the reader of many aspects of the topic
– given readers enough information to enable them to form a personal opinion on the subject

8 Which arguments in the article do you sympathise with?
After reading the article, have you changed your mind about whether or not you would eat the vegetables?
Write a short paragraph summarising your views.

14

Modern life

The aim of this unit is to focus on the following:

– skimming for main ideas and identifying specific information
– inferring information which is not clearly stated
– identifying the tone and purpose of a text
– inferring and understanding the writer's intentions and attitude

The multiple-choice exam question requires you to infer information about the writer's views and attitude which are not clearly stated.

Section A

1 One of the themes of the article in this section by Peter Ustinov is the ability of human beings to adapt to an environment which is increasingly demanding on the body and the senses.

Before you read the article, note down things in daily life which you find particularly stressful and put them in order of how stressful they are to you.

Which of the things on your list would have been unknown to former generations?

2 ⌐o The writer discusses the following themes. Look quickly through the article and decide what order they appear in. Try to take no more than two minutes.

 future frontiers attitudes to life and death
 nostalgia for the past the limits of medieval man's experience
 the fight against physical ageing

3 ⌐o The article refers to the following things:

1 the light from a fire or a candle
2 diet
3 organ transplant surgery
4 fatalism
5 thunder and cathedral music
6 television
7 aerobics
8 Aids victims
9 discotheques
10 interplanetary travel

Scan the article and find out which of the themes in 2 they are used to illustrate.

USTINOV AT LARGE
In time for a divine comedy

IN VIEW of the stress to which we are subjected, it is remarkable that we tend to live longer than our medieval ancestors. They would not have known what to make of the word "stress" unless it was used in the context of shipbuilding, architecture or the weaving of cloth.

Consider the limits of their experience. For them, as for us, the sun was the most blinding of lights. But after this natural phenomenon there was nothing brighter than a fire in the hearth, a brazier and, finally, the candle.

The working day must have been considerably shorter and the eye only subjected to the strain of trying to work by flickering candlelight. Even an eight-minute mile could not have been possible in their wildest dreams, and fun and games were limited to maypoles for the poor and jousting for the rich.

If you had given a medieval man a modern car as a form of transport, he would have panicked at first. But if he had a foolhardy nature, he might have coaxed it up to 30 kilometres per hour before crashing it into some obstacle.

Even after many lessons his reflexes would have been utterly unable to cope with the new frontiers of possibility. As for attaining the legal speed limit, the crash would merely have come sooner.

The fastest thing he would ever have been liable to see was the flight of an arrow or, perhaps, a shooting star at night – but that was so unreal as to be merely decorative. In the realm of noise there was thunder and brass instruments in the cathedral, but nothing to match the total lack of silence we suffer from today.

The sirens of fire brigades and police, with their evil cadences, would have struck panic in the medieval heart. As for the sheer assault on the nerves practised by certain discotheques, in which the volume is accompanied by psychedelic lighting – that stammering, stuttering abuse of the optic nerves – the poor friar of long ago would have believed himself prematurely in a hell, out of range of even Dante's imagination.

Television would have proved painful to him also, the succession of images being far too rapid for his comprehension. His eye would be attuned to static religious pictures or to irreverent statues, high up on church towers, depicting well-known clerical figures as gargoyles.

But these objects allow themselves to be dwelt upon by the tranquil gazer. His eye would have wandered at its own pace over the hidden detail, not been bludgeoned into involuntary surrender by a mad montage of abstractions. In other words, we probably absorb more images in a day than our ancestor would have managed in a year, most of them ill-digested, lingering in the mind only as subliminal worry-beads, recurring every now and then in the hopeless quest for interpretation.

There's no doubt about it – our bodies and our senses are pummelled in a way which would have been intolerable 600 years ago. And yet they surrendered to contagion and unhealthy living far more readily than we do.

For that reason, perhaps, death was perceived as a necessary adjunct to life. The concepts of heaven and hell, being devoutly believed in, lent a certain degree of morality to life and made death inevitable, sooner rather than later. Homeopathic medicine and herbalism were

---

4 🔊 What evidence is there in the article for the following statements? If there is no evidence, decide what the article really says.

1 The meaning of the word 'stress' has changed over the years.
2 Our medieval ancestors worked less than we do today.
3 They were less physically developed than modern man.
4 Their reflexes were under-developed because they were not regularly stimulated.
5 They were unable to see fast-moving objects.
6 Loud noises made them panic.
7 We live longer than our ancestors because our senses are continually being stimulated.
8 We are unable to interpret all the visual images our eyes absorb daily.

already far in advance of conventional medicine, but there was certainly a tendency towards fatalism which encouraged a gloomy acceptance of the worst.

There never seems to have been the almost hysterical flight before death which is apparent today, both in the sad bravery of those condemned by Aids and in the struggles of brilliant surgeons in the transplant of more and more unlikely organs into the bodies of the barely living.

Naturally, all this speaks highly for the resilience and the ingenuity of the human animal. In its contemporary form this animal is unwilling to accept the resignation of past times, and works overtime to negate the implacable rules of nature. There is no telling whether this tendency will continue.

Certainly the increased activity of today has prolonged youth far into what was once considered advanced middle age, and middle age stretches far into what was thought of as the ultimate years of life's span. Exercise, the voluntary exhaustion of the human mechanism, is partly due to the speed of life and the need for lightning reactions. The new preoccupations with diet and physical well-being, expressed in many ways from *cuisine minceur* to that orgy of hopping and skipping enjoying the typical pseudo-scientific name of aerobics, are valid reflections of the preoccupations of today.

And what lies ahead? Certain hand-picked individuals have already been introduced to the challenge of weightlessness. Eventually this may be a more general requirement, as the inhabitants of the Earth emigrate from the planet in search of pristine verities.

Incidentally, one genius this technique might have helped materially is Michelangelo, who could have knocked off the ceiling of the Sistine Chapel in a trice, instead of the age it actually took him. Many readers will still vividly remember Roger Bannister's cracking of the four-minute mile. Nowadays runners unable to qualify for the Olympics can manage this on occasions.

Even that briefest of distances, the 100 metres, is under permanent assault. These are all marks of human evolution, as is the development of sports equipment and other scientific aids to make the unbelievable possible.

And yet there must be limits to the speed of human reactions. It is a wonderful irony that speeds in the stratosphere are such that total immobility sets in, enabling astronauts to climb out into space and disentangle crossed wires.

The accidents involving formation fliers and individual warplanes suggest that the border between daring and foolhardiness is, at present, just too vague to chance. Human beings are under enormous pressure, not only from the stunning acceleration of technical development, but also from a gathering nostalgia for a past which seems so clear, so natural and so untroubled.

Is this so? How would you have enjoyed having a toothache in the 12th century? The dentist always came with a drummer to drown the patient's cries.

There's a lot to be said for the times we live in, especially once discotheques are not compulsory.

5 ☞ *Exam Question* There are a number of questions or unfinished sentences below. Choose the best answer from **A**, **B**, **C** or **D**.

1 Life in the past wasn't as stressful as life today because
- **A** people led healthier lives.
- **B** people died younger.
- **C** people's experience of life was smaller.
- **D** people's diet was poorer.

2 Life today
- **A** is immoral.
- **B** accepts the rules of nature.
- **C** does not accept death easily.
- **D** is hysterical and exhausting.

3 Why are people more concerned about their physical well-being today?
- **A** They want to prove they can live longer than their ancestors.
- **B** Because they are unwilling to resign themselves to the rules of nature.
- **C** Because it is natural instinct.
- **D** Because they don't believe in heaven and hell.

⟫➔

4 The writer believes that people today
  A live too long.
  B will continue to evolve until they meet the limits of human reactions.
  C have a dangerous lifestyle.
  D will have to achieve weightlessness.

5 What is the writer's attitude to life in the past?
  A Life was easier than it is today.
  B People were happier because they were not under so much pressure.
  C Life was not as good as present nostalgia would have us believe.
  D Religion did not help people accept the future.

EXAM TIP

Very often a writer may suggest something indirectly rather than state it directly. In this case you have to infer the information by reading between the lines. You may need to read the text carefully and notice how the writer states his or her case.

When evaluating the writer's attitude, for example, look carefully at the choice of words. The way an idea is expressed may give you a clue to the writer's attitude.

One or more of the multiple-choice questions may require you to interpret underlying meaning in a text. Questions about the writer's feelings or opinions are frequently of this type.

For questions which require you to infer information, you are unlikely to find the information stated directly and you will need to use clues scattered throughout the text in order to answer the question. A careful reading of both the questions and the text is therefore necessary. These questions usually come towards the end of a series of more straightforward questions and very often test whether you have grasped the main points of the text.

6 ⟆○ We can infer the writer's views on certain aspects of medieval and modern life by his choice or words.
Example: In the realm of noise there was thunder and brass instruments in the cathedral, but nothing to match the total lack of silence we <u>suffer</u> from today.
The word 'suffer' suggests that he considers that the lack of silence is unpleasant. Read the text carefully and underline other words and phrases which reveal the writer's views.

7 Are you nostalgic about the past?
Do you consider that life in the past was healthier and in many ways better than it is today?
Why do you think that many people become nostalgic about the past as they grow older? Is this a new phenomenon?

Section B

1 Read the opening paragraph of the article *Psychobabble*. Can you guess what it is a description of?

> OK, you're feeling unhappy. I'll tell you what: come round to my place and lie on the sofa. I'll sit on this armchair here while you say whatever comes into your head. You can ramble on for an hour, then I'll tell you time's up and charge you £35. We'll do this three times a week for four or five years, after which time you'll be no less confused than you were when you started, but I'll be £30,000 richer. How does that sound?

Now look quickly through the rest of the article and see if you were right.

2 🖥 Read the paragraph again and decide what the writer's main purpose is. You may decide there is more than one answer.

a) to shock the reader
b) to amuse the reader
c) to describe a typical analysis session
d) to criticise psychoanalysis
e) to convince the reader psychoanalysis is a waste of money

How do you think the writer is likely to answer the question at the end of the paragraph?

3 🖥 Read the rest of the article and find out how the writer answers the question.
Would you say the writer is prejudiced in any way?
Which of the answers in 2 best describes the writer's purpose in the article as a whole?

4 🔊 Find the following sentences in the article. What does each sentence comment on? Which sentences express approval and which express disapproval?

1 '… it goes without saying that his research contributed enormously to our understanding of the subconscious.'
2 'But analysis was then adopted for all sorts of psychological problems to which it was entirely unsuited.'
3 '… if your problem is morbid introspection then the worst thing you can do is spend hours talking about yourself.'
4 '… although Woody himself is living proof that you can be analysed until you are semi-comatose and still end up with your personal life in a mess.'
5 'You create new problems for yourself as fast as you solve them, and the phoney sense of progress is one of the things that makes it so addictive.'
6 '… and all you get rid of is the fee for another two years' treatment.'
7 'In America it was finally the health insurance companies who called a halt to all this madness.'
8 '… it involves a maximum of 25 sessions and sometimes just one.'
9 'So, rather than sitting quietly and letting the skeins of personal history tie you both in knots …'
10 'Brief counselling helps you actively re-engage with life.'

It sounds to me like a con trick, but people have been falling for it for almost a century. Freud effectively invented psychoanalysis in 1895, and it goes without saying that his research contributed enormously to our understanding of the subconscious. But whether analysis has any place in modern medical treatment is open to doubt. The "talking cure" which Freud and his co-worker Joseph Breuer developed in Vienna was designed specifically to uncover the cause of hysterical symptoms, in which narrow field they had a few successes. But analysis was then adopted for all sorts of psychological problems to which it was entirely unsuited. I'm told George Gershwin was psychoanalysed in the thirties by doctors hoping to find a cure for the neurological symptoms that troubled him. He died of a brain tumour at the age of 39.

Psychoanalysis was also tried as a cure for schizophrenia and mental deficiency on which it has no effect at all. It was used until very recently as a treatment for depression, which it can actually make worse – if your problem is morbid introspection then the worst thing you can do is spend hours talking about yourself.

Having failed to improve any of these conditions the analysts redirected their energies towards treating people who weren't ill at all, and here they struck gold. Such is the appeal of lying down and talking about yourself that the treatment became phenomenally popular. Woody Allen is the latest in a long line of western intellectuals whose reserves of money and self-doubt made them ideal candidates; although Woody himself is living proof that you can be analysed until you're semi-comatose and still end up with your personal life in a mess.

In their own defence, analysts will tell you now that curing you is not the purpose of the exercise. The point is simply to help people to understand themselves. But the assumption here is surely that understanding will produce change, which is highly doubtful. Any drunk driver who gets pulled over may well understand that he has behaved irresponsibly. But this understanding does not diminish the pleasure of drinking three gins and driving through town at 40 miles an hour. So what has this self-knowledge achieved?

In some psychoanalytical circles it's actually considered bad form to talk about what you'll achieve. The point is just to journey hopefully in the belief that what you discover along the way will more than compensate for the time and money spent. This was the kind of promise made in the old days by people selling *Encyclopaedia Britannica*. And it tends to be self-fulfilling because once you've bought the first few volumes or attended the first few dozen sessions you've invested far too much to admit it's a total waste of money. Getting to the end, wherever that is, becomes the only way of justifying all the effort you've put in. You must have seen the video game advertisement which goes: "Nintendo – will you ever reach the end?" And the frightening answer is: "No, you idiot, of course you won't." The game, like psychoanalysis, is potentially limitless. You create new problems for yourself as fast as you solve them, and the phoney sense of progress is one of the things that makes it so addictive.

The other thing that hooks people on analysis is the phenomenon of transference. It's common for patients in analysis to attach the powerful feelings they have for some important person in their lives to the analyst. Psychoanalysts, who expect and even encourage this, will tell you it's how the patient ultimately gets rid of those feelings, although it strikes me that the feelings are merely rehearsed in another context and all you get rid of is the fee for another two years' treatment.

In America it was finally the health insurance companies who called a halt to all this madness. Unable to keep up with the amounts being charged by psychoanalysts they finally insisted that therapists specify the length of treatment for different diagnoses. The analysts were forced to admit that treatment was open-ended and the benefits uncertain. As a result, people who want change, rather than just a long lie down, are being directed away from analysts and towards what's called "brief counselling". Like psychoanalysis this is a "talking cure", but it involves a maximum of 25 sessions and sometimes just one. The dominant psychological problems are identified right from the start and a time limit is set on sorting these out. So, rather than sitting quietly and letting the skeins of personal history tie you both in knots, the therapist intervenes to impose some kind of order on the patient's thinking. Learning from your experiences is encouraged and strategies are worked out that will stop you from repeating self-destructive behaviour.

This pragmatic approach may seem superficial to a psychoanalyst, but the fact is that however profound and mystical the workings of the mind, most of our problems arise from making the same stupid mistake over and over again. if you're going to break this cycle you need to *do* something. Brief counselling helps you actively re-engage with life. By contrast, spending five years on an analyst's couch seems like an elaborate tactic for avoiding it.

John Collee

Writers not only express meaning by what they say but also by the way they say something because of their attitude to a topic.

They may choose to express any of the following attitudes towards a topic or a person: admiration, sympathy, indifference, criticism, disapproval, contempt, etc. In order to interpret a writer's attitude in a text, you also have to decide:

– what the writer's purpose is: to amuse, criticise, present facts, etc.
– what the general tone of the text is: ironic, serious, matter of fact, etc.

If the writer's attitude is not immediately obvious, you may find it helpful to ask yourself the following questions:

– Is the text written in the first person?
– Is the writer critical: does he or she express approval or disapproval?
– Is the writer prejudiced: does the text present mainly positive points, mainly negative points or a balance of both, i.e. is it biased?
– Does the writer present facts? Does he or she comment on them?

5 🔊 **Which of these statements would the writer agree with?**

1 Psychoanalysis is a waste of money.
2 Only doctors can become analysts.
3 Freud used psychoanalysis to cure a wide variety of psychological problems.
4 Psychoanalysis is no longer used for curing mental diseases.
5 There is no end to an analysis.
6 Change in behaviour is only produced by self-knowledge.
7 Brief counselling is an honest form of 'talking cure'.
8 Psychoanalysis is a rich person's self-indulgence.

6 🔊 **How would you describe the writer's attitude towards the following?**

a) psychoanalysis
b) brief counselling

critical   indifferent   admiring   contemptuous
approving   disapproving   condemning   prejudiced
uncompromising

7 🔊 **What is the general tone of the article?**

ironic   humorous   matter of fact   passionate   serious

8 Rewrite the first paragraph of the article presenting psychoanalysis from a positive point of view.

15

Other people, other ways

The aim of this unit is to focus on the following:

– predicting what a text is about and forming an overall impression
– identifying arguments for and against
– looking for clues to text structure
– interpreting the writer's attitude

The 'gapped text' exam question requires you to reconstruct an incomplete text by inserting the missing paragraphs.

Section A

1 Are there smoking restrictions in your country or can people smoke anywhere? What are the social conventions surrounding smoking in private homes or at work?

2 📼 Look at the title of the article in this section from the *New York Times* and answer these questions.

1 What sort of *restrictions* are referred to?
2 Who are the *foreign smokers* likely to be?
3 What does the idea of a *last bastion* suggest?
4 What do you think the main idea of the article is?

Look quickly through the article and check your answers.

3 📼 Read the incomplete article and the paragraphs and find out if the writer presents arguments both for and against smoking restrictions. Or does she only present one side of the problem? What do you think the writer's attitude to these restrictions is likely to be?

Last Bastion for Foreign Smokers

Appalled by Restrictions, Visitors Take Refuge in Bistros

By LYNDA RICHARDSON

Shortly after 10 o'clock on a recent morning, a white and blue tour bus lumbered up to Caffe Lucca, a popular coffee-house in Greenwich Village, and disgorged dozens of European tourists. More than a few of them had cigarettes dangling from their lips like spare appendages.

1

"The place is full of them, and they sit and puff," said Sal Moussa, the cafe owner. "The laws are different here, and they think they are stupid laws. 'Typical Americans,' they say." Anti-smoking fervour has left America a bewildering place indeed for a foreigner who simply takes for granted the inalienable right to light up in public. And there is hardly anywhere more bewildering than New York, where some of the nation's toughest smoking restrictions may soon be expanded to include all restaurants and to ban cigarette advertising on billboards.

2

"Europeans are very stubborn," said Ze Cardosa, a general contractor from Lisbon, tossing back his head in a swirl of smoke at Caffe Lucca. "If they are just coming here to visit, if they want to smoke, they're going to smoke no matter what, especially if they are Italians or Portuguese."

3

To be regarded as a criminal, some would suggest, is better than as an insect. "I feel like a mosquito," said Marian Sanchez-Elia, a financial consultant from Buenos Aires, flailing his arms in imitation of the way Americans bat away his offensive tobacco fumes.

4

In the eyes of many foreigners, this non-smoking militancy points, more than anything else, to the extremes in American society: the same countrymen who eschew smoking and exercise obsessively are also among the unhealthiest people living. "There's always a contradiction in this country, they care about the cigarettes, but they don't care if people get fat," a 23 year-old Japanese painter commented.

5

The toughest of the European anti-smoking laws are in France. But visitors say there is little of the zealotry and Puritanism they find in America. In a country where the right to relax and smoke is considered part of the "art de vivre" – and where an estimated 40 per cent of adults and 65 per cent of those between 18 and 24 smoke – the new rules have been greeted by little more than a Gallic shrug in many cafes, bistros and brasseries.

6

While some people must suffer, others find a way to benefit. The call for a smoke-free environment has been a boon to business at the Caffe Reggio in Greenwich Village, according to the headwaiter, Jack Williams. He informs visitors of two separate sections. "I say smoking or chain-smoking?"

The eating salon is not required by law to have a non-smoking section because it seats fewer than 50 people. Half of the cafe's business caters to Japanese and European tourists who "smoke like kings and queens", Mr Williams said. At times, the waiter said he is so shrouded in cigarette fog that his clothes turn a smoky gray. "It's the truth; I've got clothes that are beyond black."

EXAM TIP

Before you do the exam question in this section you may find it useful to reread the Exam tips in Units 6, 9 and 13.

When you tackle the 'gapped' text question type don't forget to identify the type of text you are dealing with first of all. This will help you look for useful clues to links between the different paragraphs. As you read the text and paragraphs for the first time, you may find it helpful to underline words and expressions which are important for meaning. When there is no obvious chronological sequence or development of an argument, you may have to look more closely for vocabulary groups and reference words.

A Mr Cardosa, a gaunt man in a black suit, considers himself a gentleman. But having lived in the United States for some 20 years, he said American social trends strain even his well-mannered sensibilities. He is stunned at the lengths to which Americans will go, from outright orders to vicious facial expressions, to make smokers quit. "If you're smoking, they give you a dirty look. They look at you as if you're almost a criminal," Mr Cardosa said.

B "America is a land of excess; people care more about everything; their opinions are so strong. They smoke and drink in Japan and they really don't care because most people are healthy. Here, they have to care more about their health because they're eating too much junk stuff."

C The dimly lighted cafe beckons New Yorkers with the promise of dark espresso and deep conversation. But it is the blue-gray haze of cigarette smoke that makes these European tourists feel at home at the Caffe Lucca. The young people are smoking. The grandmothers are smoking. Everybody is incessantly puffing in what seems to them, alas, the last bastion for smokers in New York City.

D "In the bars, it's not respected," said Philippe Rey-Gorez, a radio journalist on holiday from Paris, as he drank his morning coffee and smoked at the Cafe Figaro in Greenwich Village. "When you go into bars to have a drink, it's impossible not to smoke. It's the place where people can meet and speak and listen to music."

E Many European countries have introduced their own restrictions. Not only are they often disregarded, they are regarded by some smokers as an invasion of American social mores.

F To foreigners who take refuge in the smoking zones of the city's bistros, cafes and restaurants, this anti-tobacco militancy is a peculiarly American bit of foolishness, emblematic of one or another flaw in the national character. These people are, after all, from countries like Portugal, France and Italy, where a cigarette and a cup of coffee or a glass of wine go together like peanut butter and jelly – and where a tendency to muse about national character is part of the national character.

G "They are completely crazy," said Mr Sanchez-Elia, as he had lunch with friends from South America the other day at Jerry's restaurant in SoHo. Mr Sanchez-Elia, wearing a black beret and leather jacket, felt immediately at home in the restaurant's smoking section, located conveniently near the bar. In other restaurants, he muttered, "You usually have to sit near the kitchen or in some back room."

4 What type of organisation does the text follow?

a) there is a chronological development
b) the writer develops an argument
c) the passage describes a situation and presents various comments on it
d) the writer presents personal views and comments on them herself

5 *Exam Question*   Read this article, then choose the best paragraph from **A–G** to fill each of the numbered gaps in the text. (There is one extra paragraph which does not belong in any of the gaps.) Try to do this question in no more than ten minutes.

6 Answer the questions.

1 Why do foreigners go to Caffe Lucca?
2 What, according to many foreigners, does the anti-tobacco militancy suggest about the American character?
3 What is one explanation given in the text for this extreme behaviour?
4 How do the Japanese differ from Americans?

7 Are you a smoker or a non-smoker? How do you feel about smoking? Write a paragraph expressing your opinions.

Section B

1 🔊 Skim through the article below. What is the topic?
Where would you expect to find this article?
What do you think the writer's intentions are? Which of the following is
he doing?

a) expressing personal views
b) telling a story
c) giving information
d) describing
e) developing an argument

2 🔊 Match the main ideas to the paragraphs.

a) The Mohana fishermen from Pakistan still live as their ancestors did 5,000 years ago.
b) The future is gloomy for the illiterate Mohana in modern Muslim Pakistan.
c) The fishermen make use of the herons' excellent eyesight to locate fish in the muddy water.
d) The Mohana fishermen use trained herons to catch fish.
e) The captured heron is trained for about two months.
f) The Mohana live on the river Indus in the isolated Sind desert area.
g) The fishermen do not breed herons but capture and train fully grown birds.
h) The carpenters and boat traders.
i) Problems both ancient and modern are making the survival of the Mohana people unlikely.
j) Despite their faith and solidarity, a miracle is needed to save their way of life.

The Bird People
ADAM BAINE

A   The Mohana fishermen of central Pakistan are a living link with some of the earliest moments of human history. Isolated from change by the inhospitability of their environment, they live a life which has barely altered in five millennia. Some call them Noah's children.

B   They live in floating villages on the banks of the Indus, in the flood plain of Sind, where for 200 miles the river cuts through what is otherwise desert wasteland. **1** ... The climate is harsh and unpredictable; the terrain desolate; the river, up to three miles wide at points, too treacherous for any but the Mohana to navigate.

C   They live as they have always lived, each person's role rigidly predetermined. There are three castes, based on the three traditional river trades: fishing, boat building and ferrying. **2** ... They fish the shallow waters at the edge of the river for carp, catfish and tortoises. This is no easy task: the alluvial currents make it all but impossible to locate the fish. The solution is to use trained herons.

D   Herons are endowed with oils on the surface of their eyes which act as colour filters. These enable them to discern the tiniest movements in the murky surface of the water and thus to detect the fish below, which they then dive for and catch. For the *shikari*, such skills mean the difference between life and death. **3** … The fisherman, following in a shallow rowing boat (*batelo*), approaches the heron, then leaps into the shallow water, trapping the fish in a conical net trap known as a *kulari*.

E   The Mohana have never bred herons in captivity. There are so many in the region that it is not necessary. **4** … The process by which they do so is particularly striking. First, a captive heron is tethered in shallow water. The fisherman, meanwhile, his head camouflaged inside a stuffed heron, hides on the riverbank some 50 yards away. Eventually, though perhaps not for many hours, a wild heron will join the tethered bird, and the fisherman can make his move. Slowly and noiselessly he swims towards the wild heron. If it turns to look at him, he stops and treads water, his head submerged in the muddy river, holding his breath. Then, with the distance narrowed to a couple of yards, he lunges forward and grabs the heron by its ankles.

F   For the next two months, the heron is trained, mostly by association with birds which have already been trained. **5** … To Europeans, the idea of training herons may seem absurd; to the Mohana, the herons are as much a part of everyday life as the river itself.

G   **6** … Above them are the *kurnangar*, or carpenters, who build both the *batelo* and the large *doondee*, or houseboats, in which the Mohana live. The latter, which are moored together to form floating villages, are made entirely of driftwood (with bamboo rivets) and can be anything up to 30ft long and 12ft wide. Wall carvings of boats exactly corresponding to these designs have been found in the ancient city of Mohenjo-Daro, dating from 3,000BC. The highest caste of all are the *mirbamar*, who ferry cargoes (most lucratively teak) to the northern and southern boundaries of the Sind. **7** …

H   Yet all three castes now face a similar fate: extinction. On the one hand, they are threatened by problems almost as ancient as their own traditions. They have to pay tribute – up to half their incomes – to their feudal landlords, the Zamidar, who own the shores of the river. What remains is all too often plundered by dacoits – bandits from the jungles of northern Sind. **8** … Seven dams recently constructed between the Punjab and southern Sind have not only closed trading routes for the *mirbamar* but also killed many of the migratory fish on which the *shikari* depend. In addition, provoked by the dacoits' habit of commandeering Mohana boats to further their criminal activities, Pakistani police have confiscated whole fleets of them, thus leaving an already impoverished people with still less means of support.

I   The Mohana civilisation has survived for 5,000 years, but there are many observers who predict that it will not last another 20. The Mohana are too cut off from the mainstream of Pakistani life to thrive in the late 20th century. **9** … Their blend of Hindu and animist beliefs (they worship Khwaja Khizir, an 18th century tribal leader now revered as the reincarnated god of the Indus) does not endear them to the rest of the population, most of whom are devoutly Muslim. Yet without a measure of sympathy or support from modern Pakistan, their problems can only intensify.

J   In the 17th century, the Mohana had some 13,000 boats. Today they have scarcely 4,000. **10** … Centuries of persecution have forged an unshakeable collective solidarity, a refusal to contemplate change and a deep faith in the ultimate salvation of the tribe as a whole. The central myth of Mohana tradition involves an ancestor named Noah (pronounced as in English, but with no proven link to the Old Testament) who called the entire tribe into an ark-shaped boat and piloted them to safety. Struggling to stay afloat in a flood of troubles, the Mohana are praying for a similar miracle to save them today.

STUDY TIP

Although you probably don't usually focus on the way sentences are linked together to form coherent 'lumps of text', you may find this useful if you are faced with a particularly complex passage.

For example, if you cannot grasp the meaning of a paragraph but are familiar with all the vocabulary, you are probably having trouble understanding the way the sentences relate to one another.

In order to understand how sentences are organised into paragraphs, you need to recognise both the way the sentences are linked together and also the function of the sentences in the context.

3 ⌨ **In the article, some sentences are missing. Choose suitable sentences from the list below to fill the spaces and write the correct number in each space.**

i) It is an almost magical process, developed and refined over some 5,000 years.

ii) A trained heron, instead of diving, will stand stock still above a fish or shoal.

iii) Yet it is difficult to imagine them breaking with their traditions and moving to a life on the land.

iv) On the other hand, they now face modern hazards.

v) Despite their skills, the *shikari*, who account for nearly two-thirds of the Mohana people, are the lowliest of the three castes.

vi) Few other living creatures survive there.

vii) Nomadic and illiterate, they make no obvious contribution to the economy.

viii) The fishermen, or *shikari*, are the most unusual.

ix) Instead, they capture fully grown wild specimens and train them.

x) They are the smallest caste but own most of the community's wealth.

4 ⚷ Underline the words, expressions or ideas which helped you decide where the sentences go.

5 ⚷ Find the words or expressions in the passage and answer the questions.

1 'The climate is *harsh* ...' Is it likely to be a pleasant or an unpleasant climate to live in?
2 '*murky*' Is the water clear or is it dirty?
3 'a captive heron is *tethered* ...' Is it in a cage or held with a rope?
4 'he *lunges* forward ...' Does he move quickly or slowly?
5 'to *thrive*' Does this mean to do well or to survive?

6 Look through the article again and write down words you can use to talk about rivers and river life.

7 ⚷ Why do you think the writer focuses on the fishermen and not on the other castes? What does the article tell us about the writer's attitude to the Mohana people? Which of the following do you think it reveals?

regret   optimism   pessimism   lack of concern
a neutral attitude

8 Do you know of any other traditional civilisations who still live as their ancestors did? Do you think that traditional civilisations such as the Mohana can survive in the modern world?

Do you think it is desirable to help them continue their traditional way of life or should governments be doing more to integrate them into modern life?

16

The world of work

The aim of this unit is to focus on the following:

– understanding main ideas and retrieving specific information

– dealing with difficult vocabulary and, in particular, with figurative language

– inferring and understanding the writer's opinions

The multiple-choice exam questions require you to infer information which is not clearly stated.

Section A

1 The theme of this section is the office environment. Look at the different types of offices in the pictures above and for each one write down two or three advantages and disadvantages. Which office type would you prefer to work in?

The eternal coffee break

Computers and electronic communications are allowing many people to use their homes as offices. But offices will never disappear entirely. Instead, the office of the future may become like home.

AMERICAN managers who want to get more out of their white-collar workforce will be in for a shock if they seek advice from Frank Becker, a professor at Cornell University who studies the patterns of office work.

Mr Becker is one of a group of academics and consultants trying to make companies more productive by linking new office technology to a better understanding of how employees work. The forecasts of a decade ago – that computers would increase office productivity, reduce white-collar payrolls and help the remaining staff to work better – have proved much too hopeful. Mr Becker, who unfortunately calls himself an "organisational ecologist", is trying to find out why the huge sums of money spent on office automation have produced such disappointing results. He is leading a two-year study on offices called "Workscape 21". Sponsored by Cornell, the study is financed by firms in America, Japan, Britain and Holland.

Even before completing the study, Mr Becker has firm ideas about how the office of the future should look. Technology, better communications, rising inner-city land costs (once today's property bust is over) and the trials of commuting will, he predicts, prompt more workers to split time between a central office, a computer-equipped home office and perhaps a satellite office in a suburban business park.

Even those few workers based at the central office will be more mobile, moving between different work stations as their tasks change, taking their mobile telephones with them. This will cut the amount of wasted office space, says Mr Becker. It will also improve communications between employees, by pushing them out of the tight and unchanging circle of people who sit nearby.

Mr Becker predicts that the central office will become mainly a place where workers from satellite and home-based offices meet to discuss ideas and to reaffirm their loyalty to fellow employees and the company. This will require new thoughts about the layout of office buildings. Now, spaces for copying machines, coffee rooms, meetings and reception areas usually come second to the offices in which people spend most of the day working. Mr Becker sees these common areas gradually becoming the heart of an office. He even believes that many central offices will come to resemble a hotel lobby or somebody's home – a disturbing thought, that, for people who find in the calm of the office a refuge from the rigours of family life.

Managers, says Mr Becker, will also have to abandon their long-cherished notion that a productive employee is an employee that can be seen. Appearing on time and looking busy will soon become irrelevant. Technology and new patterns of office use will make companies judge people by what they do, not by where they spend their time.

That does not mean the end of the office, just its transformation into a social centre. Thomas Allen, a professor of management at Massachusetts Institute of Technology, has studied communication patterns between people, in the admittedly artificial environment of research laboratories. His less-than-startling conclusion is that people talk to each other more when they work in close proximity. Workers on different floors might as well be in different buildings, so rarely do they see one another. Because buildings are seldom designed with employee-to-employee contact in mind, co-workers may barely know someone a few yards away, even though they have related jobs.

To show how this can be changed, Mr Allen has helped one pharmaceutical firm to establish an experimental office designed to get chemists and biologists to talk more to each other. A similar bunch of employees, serving as a control group, is occupying a more conventional building. The two groups will be compared for such things as the time they take to complete reports and the rate at which they find new chemical compounds.

New ideas about offices are catching on elsewhere. IBM's British division will soon have all 1,000 of its headquarter's employees working in "non-territorial" offices – places where they have no desk to call their own. And in California TRW and GTE are trying to help employees cope with traffic problems and work more efficiently by setting up satellite offices. Digital Equipment Corp's subsidiary in Finland has equipped offices with reclining chairs and stuffed sofas to make them more comfortable and conducive to informal conversations and the swapping of ideas. Companies such as Apple and General Electric are experimenting along similar lines.

Steelcase, a manufacturer of office furniture, is one of the firms keenest to experiment with new office layouts and designs. The company's research centre in Grand Rapids, Michigan, is a $111m building completed in 1989. It is designed around a series of office "neighbourhoods" that put marketing, manufacturing and design people close to each other so that they can find it easier to discuss ideas and solve problems. Employees on different floors can see one another through glass, and easily go from floor to floor via escalators.

Top managers work in a cluster of offices that are wrapped around an atrium in the middle of the building, rather than occupying the usual suite of top-floor offices. They can see, and be seen by, the people they manage. Mr Allen, who worked as a consultant to Steelcase and argued vigorously for placing the bosses' offices in the middle of the building, believes it will improve managers' chances of bumping into the people they lead. "Who knows," he says, "they might even talk to them."

Enriching as it is to be constantly under the gaze of your superiors, Steelcase employees are also rather keen on 14 "think-tanks" located on the sixth floor of the pyramid. Intended for intense, individual work, these small offices are equipped with a computer, but no telephone. Available on a first-come, first-served basis, these havens are rarely unoccupied. Sometimes even the most communicative employee just wants to be left alone.

2 🔑 The points below are discussed in the article. Look quickly through the article and decide what order they appear in. Take no more than five minutes to do this.

1 new office designs
2 central and satellite offices
3 individual work and isolation
4 office productivity and automation
5 the central office as a meeting place
6 the bosses' offices
7 staff mobility within the office
8 office layout and communication

3 🔑 Find out who or what the following are:

Mr Becker   Thomas Allen   Steelcase

What aspects of the working environment are they trying to improve?

4 🔑 Read the article and decide whether the statements below are true or false.

1 Office designs should reflect the way people work.
2 Forecasters of ten years ago predicted a sharp increase in office staff.
3 In the future more people will work at home.
4 Frank Becker advocates a more comfortable working environment.
5 The writer suggests that land prices in urban areas will tend to decrease in the future.
6 Most present-day offices were designed with inter-staff communication in mind.
7 Common areas will be phased out in favour of more comfortable offices.
8 Increased communication between biologists and chemists is expected to result in a faster discovery rate.
9 Steelcase manufactures and sells furniture.
10 At the Steelcase headquarters senior executives have their offices on the top floor.

5 🔑 Write a sentence in answer to the following questions:

1 How has automation affected office productivity over the last decade?
2 What are the main drawbacks of traditional office layouts?
3 What is likely to be the main function of the central office in the future?
4 How are the new office designs likely to affect communication between workers?
5 What are the disadvantages of placing top managers in the traditional top-floor offices?

6 🔑 *Exam Question*   Read the article from a business magazine and answer questions **1–5** by choosing **A**, **B**, **C** or **D**.

1 How has automation affected office productivity over the last decade?
   A Computers have improved efficiency.
   B Office productivity has improved less than expected.
   C Automation has had little effect on productivity.
   D The number of office workers has been significantly reduced.

2 What is the main drawback of traditional office layouts?
   A Employees cannot see one another.
   B Communication is not easy.
   C The boss's office is always on the top floor.
   D They are uncomfortable.

3 Mr Becker believes that the central office of the future will
   A have more staff working there than today.
   B only be used by managers.
   C become an important meeting place for workers.
   D gradually disappear and be replaced by home-based offices.

4 What does Mr Allen hope to demonstrate at the experimental office he has helped to design?
   A Chemists and biologists can work together in the right surroundings.
   B Building design affects communications and efficiency.
   C Researchers work better in conventional buildings.
   D Increased employee-to-employee contact stimulates competition.

5 Why has Steelcase placed its top managers' offices in the middle of the building?
   A So the managers can get to know their employees better.
   B So they can supervise their staff more efficiently.
   C Because they can solve management problems better if they are grouped together.
   D To provide space for the 'think tanks' on the top floor.

EXAM TIP

A number of different reading strategies are tested by multiple-choice questions. Some are straightforward comprehension questions where you are expected to identify stated information. Others require you to read between the lines and infer the writer's meaning which may be expressed indirectly. Yet others ask you to identify and interpret opinions and the writer's attitude. The final questions in the series are often designed to test understanding of overall meaning.

The multiple-choice question may therefore be more complex than it appears and in all cases requires a close reading of the text. The incorrect options or *distractors* in the multiple-choice question can be of several types:

– untrue or contrary to what is stated in the text
– not mentioned in the text (although they may be true)
– only partially true
– true but irrelevant to the question

The correct option will be the only one which is *entirely* true for a *given* text and *relevant* to the question.

7 Compare your answers in 5 with your choices in 6.

8 Do you think that many of the ideas promoted by Frank Becker and Thomas Allen are likely to become commonplace in the future?
Which do you find the most appealing?
What do you dislike about your own working/studying environment?
How could you improve it?

Section B

1 The theme of this section is meetings. Look at the picture on page 120 and say what the object of the meeting might be. What are the different participants doing? How effective do you think the meeting is?

Think about these questions:

- Do you ever go to meetings? If so, how often?
- What sort of meetings have you attended?
- When was the last time you went to a meeting?
- Can you describe a meeting you have attended? Think about: number of participants; object; length; atmosphere; decisions made.
- Would you say that the meeting was efficient or was a lot of time wasted?

2 Look at the title of the article on the next page. In what situation would you expect to receive this in answer to a request? Read the sub-heading and the first paragraph. Note down a few points you think the writer may mention in the article.

3 ⏻ Read the article and find out whether the writer generally approves or disapproves of meetings.

STUDY TIP

The text in this section is more difficult than many in this book. One reason for this is that it contains quite a lot of specialised vocabulary. But the main difficulty is probably the figurative language which the writer uses throughout the article.

Read this sentence from the text: *The second version claims that meetings provide little more than strategic sites for corporate gladiators to perform before the organisational emperors.* The words which are underlined are examples of figurative language: the meeting room is implicitly compared to an arena where gladiators, i.e. members of a managerial team, fight before emperors, i.e. important senior executives.

If you aren't familiar with figurative language you may be confused by the use of words such as *gladiator* and *emperor* which have no obvious connection with the world of management. It is therefore important to bear in mind that a word or expression may not always be taken at face value. It may be necessary to go beyond its obvious or literal meaning and look for a figurative meaning which enables you to interpret the text and understand the meaning in context.

Sorry, he's in conference

How much of your time at work today will be spent at meetings?

How much of that time was *really* spent working?

Jean-Louis Barsoux on an essential part of management

Managers spend a great deal of their time in meetings. According to Henry Mintzberg, in his book, *The Nature of Managerial Work*, managers in large organisations spend only 22 per cent of their time at their desks, but 69 per cent of their time in meetings. So what are the managers doing in those meetings?

There have conventionally been two answers. The first is the academic version: managers are co-ordinating and controlling, making decisions, solving problems and planning. This interpretation has been largely discredited because it ignores the social and political forces at work in meetings.

The second version claims that meetings provide little more than strategic sites for corporate gladiators to perform before the organisational emperors. This perspective is far more attractive, and has given rise to a large, and often humorous, body of literature on gamesmanship and posturing in meetings.

It is, of course, true that meeting rooms serve as shop windows for managerial talent, but this is far from the whole truth. The suggestion that meetings are essentially battle grounds is misleading since the *raison d'être* of meetings has far more to do with comfort than conflict. Meetings are actually vital props, both for the participants and the organisation as a whole.

For the organisation, meetings represent recording devices. The minutes of meetings catalogue the changing face of the organisation, at all levels, in a more systematic way than do the assorted memos and directives which are scattered about the company. They enshrine the minutiae of corporate history, they itemise proposed actions and outcomes in a way which makes one look like the natural culmination of the other.

The whole tenor of the minutes is one of total premeditation and implied continuity. They are a sanitised version of reality which suggests a reassuring level of control over events. What is more, the minutes record the debating of certain issues in an official and democratic forum, so that those not involved in the process can be assured that the decision was not taken lightly.

As Doug Bennett, an administrative and finance manager with Allied Breweries, explains: "Time and effort are *seen* to have

4 ☞ Match the phrases below with their meaning in the context.

1 *enshrine the minutiae of corporate history*
2 *buttress their status*
3 *earn their corn*
4 *round up the strays*

A work hard for a living
B assert personal importance
C reprimand those who disregard decisions.
D record the details of company activity
E become a burden
F make everyone comply with company policy
G maintain other people's favourable opinions

The underlined words and expressions are unusual in the context. In what context would you expect to find them?
You can use a dictionary to help you.

been invested in scrutinising a certain course of action."

Key individuals are also seen to have put their names behind that particular course of action. The decision can therefore proceed with the full weight of the organisation behind it, even if it actually went through "on the nod". At the same time, the burden of responsibility is spread, so that no individual takes the blame should disaster strike.

Thus, the public nature of formal meetings confers a degree of legitimacy on what happens in them. Having a view pass unchallenged at a meeting can be taken to indicate consensus.

However, meetings also serve as an alibi for inaction, as demonstrated by one manager who explained to his subordinates: "I did what I could to prevent it – I had our objections minuted in two meetings." The proof of conspicuous effort was there in black and white.

By merely attending meetings, managers buttress their status, while non-attendance can carry with it a certain stigma. Whether individual managers intend to make a contribution or not, it is satisfying to be considered one of those whose views matter. Ostracism, for senior managers, is not being invited to meetings.

As one cynic observed, meetings are comfortingly tangible: "Who on the shop floor really believes that managers are working when they tour the works? But assemble them behind closed doors and call it a meeting and everyone will take it for granted that they are hard at work." Managers are being seen to earn their corn.

Meetings provide managers with another form of comfort too – that of familiarity. Meetings follow a set format: exchanges are ritualised, the participants are probably known in advance, there is often a written agenda, and there is a chance to prepare. Little wonder then, that they come as welcome relief from the upheaval and uncertainty of life outside the meeting room.

Managers can draw further comfort from the realisation that their peers are every bit as bemused and fallible as themselves. Meetings provide constant reminders that they share the same problems, preoccupations and anxieties, that they are all in the same boat. And for those who may be slightly adrift, meetings are ideal occasions for gently pulling them round.

As Steve Styles, the process control manager (life services) at Legal & General, puts it: "The mere presence of others in meetings adds weight to teasing or censure and helps you to 'round up the strays'." Such gatherings therefore provide solace and direction for the management team – a security blanket for managers.

Meetings do serve a multitude of means as well as ends. They relieve managerial stress and facilitate consensus. For the organisation, they have a safety-net-cum-rubber-stamping function without which decisions could not progress, much less gather momentum. In short, meetings are fundamental to the well-being of managers and organisations alike.

5 ☞ Find the following expressions and phrases in the article. What are the meanings out of context (literal meanings)? Now decide what they mean in the context (figurative meanings).

Example: *shop windows* – a shop window is where things sold in a shop are put on display to attract customers. In the text these refer to the meeting rooms which are described as places where managers can perform, i.e. show off their ability in order to impress their superiors.

Write similar definitions for the following expressions and phrases:

1 'battle grounds'
2 'in black and white'
3 'the shop floor'
4 'a security blanket'
5 'safety-net-cum-rubber-stamping function'

6 **-0** *Exam Question*   Answer questions **1–5** by choosing **A, B, C** or **D**. Try to do this question in no more than ten minutes.

1 Why are the minutes of meetings important for a company?
  A They provide a clear history of the firm and its evolution.
  B They concentrate scattered memos and directives in one synthetic document.
  C They reflect decision making and control over company life.
  D They record any individual disagreement with company decisions.

2 Why do managers consider it important to be invited to meetings?
  A They can impress their superiors.
  B All the important company decisions are taken at meetings.
  C It makes them feel that their opinions are of importance to others.
  D They can share problems and anxieties.

3 According to shop-floor workers, where do managers really work hard?
  A at their desks
  B in meetings
  C on visits to company production areas
  D on business trips

4 Why are meetings comforting for the managers who participate in them?
  A They can show off their talents.
  B They make them feel they belong to a team.
  C They are a welcome break from daily routine.
  D They are a useful alibi for inaction.

5 What, according to the writer, are the essential functions of meetings?
  A planning and controlling company activities
  B reassuring managers and conferring legitimacy on decisions
  C asserting authority and judging one's peers
  D sharing problems and censuring mistakes

7 Look at the article again and write down ten or more useful words or expressions that you can use to talk about the business world. You can use a dictionary.

Answer key

Unit 1 Foundation unit

1 b You probably guessed it was not from a newspaper because of the layout of the text, or from an advertisement because of the style of the language (there are no words encouraging you to buy the exam or adjectives describing its exceptional qualities). It is unlikely to be from an exam paper because it describes the exam itself in detail.

Remember that the layout, style of language and topic can help you decide where a text comes from.

2 B7 C8 D1 F4 G9 H2 I5

3 Louise has not yet taken FCE so she probably isn't at the right level. Julia might be at the right level if she has done seven years of English, but we can't tell until her level is checked at the beginning of the CAE preparation course. The CAE exam is probably suitable for both Sato and Reza because their level is OK and they need a more practical, less literary test of their language competence.

5 1 This sentence ending has a dash so it goes at the end of the list of reading strategies. It also has a full stop, while the others have semi-colons. Punctuation conventions probably helped you here.

2 This is about the text types used in the exam, so the subject matter gives you a rough idea, and the discourse marker *including* suggests it goes after *a wide range of text types and sources*.

3 This has *than* in it (so the clause structure requires it to go with a comparison) and *to* (so the clause structure requires it to go with a verb + infinitive construction). It comes after *required to perform a given task*.

4 This has a relative clause with *which*, and the subject matter is to do with the exam itself, so it goes after *undesirable in an examination*.

6 We can infer that the texts may be quite long *(the processing of large amounts of text)*, and that there is a variety of types *(of different types, a*

wide range of text types and sources).
The vocabulary will probably not be graded *(candidates should not expect the texts ... to include only words they are familiar with)*.
References to *real time*, *quickly* and *accurately* suggest there won't be much time for the Reading paper.
Reference to the tasks set in the exam is rather vague: the text talks about *processing* texts, and *information-transfer techniques and tasks*. We can infer that the answer sheet is a test in its own right and requires special training.

7 1 False (You only write your own name.)
2 True
3 True
4 False (There is only one answer for each question.)
5 False (You can only use an eraser.)
6 False (You shouldn't write either.)
7 True
8 False (No space is provided on the OMR sheet for full, written answers: all the questions have one letter answers.)

Unit 2 Survival

Section A

1 c The layout and topic probably helped you to decide.

2 c The leaflet is designed for boat owners. It is distributed by the Canadian Coast Guard.

3 1B 2B 3A 4C 5G 6J 7B 8A

4 1H 2I 3A 4B 5C 6E 7F

5 1 False *(Children are particularly vulnerable to cold water.)*
2 True
3 False *(... they cool slightly faster due to their usually small body size.)*
4 False *(Results show that the person swimming ... when holding still.)*

5 False *(… under no circumstances should they (alcoholic beverages) be given …)*
6 True
7 False *(Children are particularly vulnerable … because they are smaller …)*
8 False *(Cardiac arrest is the usual cause of death …)*
9 True
10 True

6 Suggested answers:
1 You shouldn't attempt to swim. You should adopt the anti-drowning technique of treading water.
2 You should all sit on the overturned boat and huddle together to keep warm.
3 You should put the lifejacket on the child and all huddle together. If one of you is a very good swimmer, you could try to reach the shore. The dilemma here is to decide who should wear the lifejacket: if the swimmer wears it, he or she will have a better chance of reaching the shore and therefore alerting rescue boats, but the chances of the child surviving are lessened.

Section B

3 1 the honeymoon   2 all at sea   3 adjusting
4 acceptance

4 b   The writer is American.

5 1 effect   2 effect   3 effect   4 advice
5 advice

6 1 acceptable   2 less delightful   3 confused
4 people who've been in America a long time
5 be depressed

7 1 True
2 No evidence (The writer says that this is how it appeared when we were children; later she says that right and wrong are not meaningful terms in cultural matters.)
3 True
4 True
5 No evidence (The writer suggests that weak family ties and the fast pace may be things you dislike, and freedom and opportunity may be things you like.)
6 True
7 No evidence (The writer says at the beginning that she came back from Italy homesick after a year's stay; at the end she says that within six months or a year of arrival, you should be moving into acceptance.)

Unit 3 Consumer issues

Section A

2 c

3 1E 2G 3C 4H 5D 6A 7F 8B

4 1D 2E 3G 4A 5F 6C 7B 8H

5 Suggested answers:
– own label products are placed on the left of main brand products
– known value items are low priced
– known value items are scattered about the store
– well-stocked shelves
– lighting adapted to products displayed
– aisle width calculated to slow people down
– popular products placed on both sides of an aisle
– a variety of high profit convenience foods

6 1 They are not the only means of watching people; in addition, employees discreetly watch shoppers.
2 They are the main priority, everything is designed to increase them.
3 So the customer will see the store label first.
4 On the contrary, they are scattered about the store.
5 Difficult to find.
6 More time.
7 On the contrary, you have to move from one side to the other to find what you want.

Section B

3 b

5 1 *Anybody who paid $2,250 for 100 shares when McDonald's was floated in 1965 would have been a shrewd investor.*
2 *The burger, reviled by environmentalists …*
3 *… where its image as an icon of Americana makes it hugely popular …*
4 *… so the focus of environmental concern has switched to the amount of packaging used.*

5 *Our testers, undeterred by any such concerns …*

6 praise: tasty cheese, soft bread, soft meat, crisp(y) vegetables, chewy meat
   criticise: cold vegetables, boring hamburger, greasy meat, dry bread, bitter cheese, rough bread, hard pickles, chewy bread, uncooked slab of cheese, salty meat

7 1a 2b 3a 4b 5b 6a

Unit 4 Transport

Section A

2 a) the traditional image of charter flights is negative; only people not rich enough to travel on a scheduled flight choose charters
   b) this negative image no longer reflects reality; charters have greatly improved all aspects of their services

3 All the features are mentioned.

5 1F 2I 3G 4J 5A 6H 7D

6 1 False *(… have been quietly bringing the quality of their services into line with the best of the scheduled carriers.)*
   2 True *(… enabling airlines to sell seats to tour operators for less in real terms than 10 years ago.)*
   3 True *(… about 140 planes chasing a diminishing market.)*
   4 True *(A charter airline makes money by packing in people.)*
   5 True *(Europe's skies are still governed by archaic technology.)*
   6 True *(Nor can you have the flexibility of an unrestricted ticket.)*
   7 False *(There is no business-class option on a charter flight.)*
   8 False *(Their advertising costs are minimal by comparison.)*

7 1a 2b 3b 4 no 5a 6b

Section B

1 b *'a prayer'* was probably the clue that helped you decide it was about the dangers of cycling.

2 A

3 Possible opening sentences: b, d, e, i, l, n

4 **Suggested answers:**
   A: b, e   B: a, c, g, h, j, m   C: d, k

5 1i 2l 3g 4k 5m 6j 7c 8n 9a 10f
   11d 12e 13b 14h

6 1b 2b 3a 4a 5b

7 1 True *(… the local authority is trying to ban bicycles from the city centre.)*
   2 True *(…90 per cent of cycle casualties occur on busy main roads.)*
   3 False *(… only the brave, foolish or gas-masked couriers venture into the traffic.)*
   4 True *(Drivers turn into pigs …   Even the most well-meaning motorist is unaware of bicycles …)*
   5 True *(… you are forced to breathe in the noxious gases.   … pumping heavy metals into cyclists' lungs …)*
   6 True *(Many local authorities now operate a reimbursement policy …   Many local authorities now have bicycle working parties …)*
   7 False *(Only Greece, with 0.2 deaths per 100,000 has a lower fatality rate.)*

Unit 5 Travel

Section A

1 c It is probably an extract from a travel brochure. It may also be an advertisement from a magazine.

2 Beijing – Badaling – Shanghai – Suzhou – Nanjing – Wuhan – Chongqing – Xian – Giulin – Hong Kong

3 1C 2E 3F 4D 5G 6H 7F 8C 9C
   10F 11C 12G 13A 14B 15B

Section B

3 1I 2F 3E 4F 5K 6G 7A 8H

5 the Lonely Planet and Rough Guides
The writer appreciates both guides.

6 1 the independent, young, budget and Green
(ecologically aware) traveller
2 the more affluent independent traveller
3 uncomplicated, no worries hedonism
4 to limit tourist pollution by deliberately
omitting certain unspoilt places from the
guides
5 the Rough Guide

7 1 & 2 *next front, battle* and *tanks* are words
usually used to talk about war. In the text they
refer to the commercial battle between the
Lonely Planet guides and the Rough Guides.
next front refers to the next commercial battle,
the TV series. *the other's lawn* refers to the
countries that each guide originally
concentrated on.
3 India and Australia. Formerly Lonely Planet
guides were the best guides to India and
Australia. Now the Rough Guides are
publishing guides to these countries.

Unit 6 Large-scale art

Section A

2 1 The life and work of the Bulgarian sculptor
Christo.
2 The article probably appeared in a newspaper
because it is very general and does not focus in
detail on artistic aspects.

3 a and c

4 1F 2A 3F 4C 5G 6B

5 born in 1935
In the early 1950s
while he was working
in 1957 he left for Austria
he went to Paris
he spent almost ten years
In later years
now
he seems *(use of present tense)*

6 1 the repressive Stalinist world of communist
Bulgaria
2 his art
3 his holiday job arranging fields and farm
buildings to create the illusion of prosperity
4 because the eastern bloc was unsympathetic to
modern art
5 to Paris
6 his work has been exhibited in Sofia and he has
been invited to work there
7 to wrap the mausoleum in Sofia
8 because he was hurt that his fellow
countrymen didn't stay in touch with him
during the Cold War

Section B

2 descriptive

3 c, d, e, f, g

4 between June and September 1971, the following
year, in the Eighties, in 1990, in 1992, in
January 1993, the summer of 1993, in April
1994, now

5 1D 2I 3A 4E 5B 6H 7G 8C

6 1 His artistic vision of writing the name of things
on the things themselves as a statement of the
obvious.
2 His neighbour's field near Stratford-upon-
Avon.
3 The figure of the swan.
4 The negative image of the zebra made by
burning straw and by laying plastic on the
ground to bleach the grass.
5 'Thieves of Time' (two magpies).
6 The image of the brown meadow butterfly.
7 The project 'All in a Day's Work'.

Unit 7 Children and education

Section A

1 Suggested answers:
1 A camp where teenagers can learn about the
stock market during their holidays.
2 They prefer to play the stock market than do
more usual teenager activities like swimming.
3 Who these kids are; why they choose this type
of holiday; what they learn about at the camp;
what the aims of this type of camp are.

2 1 They are not sane or normal children. The writer implies that sane teenagers would prefer to spend their holiday swimming.

2 He is a good teacher.

3 This suggests that the writer disapproves of the course and imagined that the sort of children who would participate are likely to be 'spoilt brats': unpleasant children.

4 Gerard Di Santo II's father, Gerard Di Santo I.

5 The writer implies that it is a pity wider moral dilemmas are not discussed on the course.

3 1d 2a 3b 4c 5e

4 1D 2G 3F 4C 5D 6A 7E 8B 9G

Section B

1 **Suggested answers:**

1 It is likely to be about the problems and special needs of very intelligent children.

2 & 3 The extracts in italics have probably been made by people interviewed for the article, and suggest a number of ideas that are probably developed in the article: high ability children may need special attention; private schools are not necessarily the answer; going through the system faster than other children does not necessarily cause social problems for these children.

2 1 Mike Turner: of the National Association for Curriculum Enrichment and Extension

2 Dr Chitham: educational consultant for the National Association for Gifted Children

3 Dr Chitham

4 Dr Chitham

5 Mike Turner

6 Dr Chitham

3 1g 2h 3a 4e 5d 6i

4 b) Dr Chitham *('They can look around for a more suitable school.')*

c) Mr Turner *(In the case of sport or music, special provision may have to be made out of school.)*

f) Dr Chitham *('... our long-term aim is to try to change the climate of opinion in schools.')*

Unit 8 The oceans

Section A

3 True: 1, 3, 4, 5, 6
False: 2, 7, 8

4 1A 2C 3A 4B 5B

5 warming, currents, climatic, oceans, tropics, polar, equator, research, data, valleys, energy, seabed, direction

Section B

1 1 A: the scientific use of shoes which accidentally fell off a ship
B: a report on Japanese trainers which have crossed the Pacific

2 Nike trainers are floating around in the sea.
They are crossing the Pacific Ocean.
They are washing ashore in the US.
They have been in the sea since spring 1990.

3 A says there are 80,000 trainers, B 40,000.

4 A: a fleet of message-bearing bottles
B: a Japanese armada, secret invaders, a flotilla. The image is that of a military invasion evoking a historic event in the past.

5 The focus is on the scientific uses that can be made of accidental events. This suggests that the article will probably emphasise the scientific aspect of the shoe spill.

2 B – Text 1; A – Text 2

3 – Most of Text 2 is concerned with the scientific aspect and the monitoring of ocean currents. Only the last paragraph reports an anecdote irrelevant to science.

Text 1 is more interested in what happens to the trainers, and gives detailed anecdotes about the beachcombers and the resistance of the shoes.

– The vocabulary used in Text 1 is complex and varied. The writer uses imagery: an invading army (see activity 1); words more normally used for living things are used to describe the trainers: survived, resilience, appearing, bobbing, fate, prowess; there is play on words: sole/soul, circuit training; the use of unusual adjectives: *watery* fate, *sartorial* requisites, *briny* immersion, *multicoloured* trainers, *well-heeled* landing army, *thriving* economy, *weather-proofing* prowess.

The vocabulary of Text 2 is straightforward. There are few images and adjectives. Apart from the last paragraph, the article is a straightforward report.
- Both texts refer to the same scientists. Text 2 introduces them both and their functions at the beginning of the text. In Text 1 they are mentioned almost incidentally in different parts of the article.
- Both texts include quotes from the scientists: in Text 1 they are not about their work, in Text 2, all but one are about their work.

4 1 they have been reselling them
2 a storm struck the ship
3 the shores of Oregon
4 they appeared farther south than would normally have been expected
5 they weren't interested
In Text 2, 3 is developed in more detail, 5 is not mentioned.

5 c Text 1 probably appeared in a daily newspaper. The article is about Nike shoes and is presented in an amusing style.
a Text 2 probably appeared in a general science magazine. It focuses on the scientific aspect of the shoe spill but it does not go into great detail, which would be expected in a specialist journal.

Unit 9 Memorable incidents

Section A

1 narrative

2 1 The story of a shark attack on a small motor boat.
2 On a lagoon in Mozambique.
3 The writer's parents, his brother Stewart, a girl called Margo, local fishermen.
4 A shark attacks the family's boat.
5 They are taken on board a fishing boat.

4 1D 2G 3A 4H 5B 6E 7C

5 1 the shark
2 the writer, his brother, Margo
3 that took them on board
4 the incident
5 the dead shark

6 the story
7 what looked like a shark
8 of the shark attack
9 the motor on their rowing boat
10 the shark

Section B

1 1 The writer has his suitcase stolen from a motel room.
2 In a motel in Texas, USA.
3 He doesn't get his suitcase back.

2 Action: 1, 3, 5, 8, 9, 11
Comment: 2, 4, 6, 7, 10, 12

4 1G 2E 3A 4D 5B 6H 7C

5 *Just to sit in that room depressed me, …*
The thought was intolerable, …
I plaintively asked the police.
… I tried to calm myself.
… the sense of outrage, violation …
… a sickening desolation …

6 – the clerk: nothing
– the security man: he was sympathetic at first but he went away when the writer accused the hotel of having no security
– the first driver: *shaking his head in disbelief, …* he was amazed but did as he was asked because he didn't want the writer to give his number to the police
– the second driver: he was unco-operative and refused to open his boot
– the cop: he was horrified that the writer had been naive enough to stop cars

Unit 10 Cultural issues

Section A

1 Breton, Frisian, English
Breton and Frisian are minority languages.

2 1D 2F 3C 4E 5I 6K 7L 8H

3 A: the number of people who understand Breton but who don't necessarily speak it
B: the number of inhabitants of countries where English is the official language
G: the population of the Breton region of France

4 **Suggested answers:** Texts 1 and 2: a; Text 3: b

5 English is already the European *lingua franca*.
It is spoken in countries all over the world.
It is the official language in many countries.
There is no English academy to prevent the language developing.
It is less formal and more flexible than French or German.
It symbolises modern consumerism, prosperity and material progress and hope.
It represents the cheapest solution for overcoming language barriers.

Section B

1 a

2 1 True (indirectly stated: *hands on your lap, dear*)
2 False
3 False
4 False
5 True (indirectly stated: *... and you'd better tip the nurses, too*)
6 False
7 True (indirectly stated: *... as in the States*)
8 True (indirectly stated: *It's no good telling a Turk to celebrate his birthday and not his name day*)
9 True (indirectly stated: *... or trying to make an Italian child ... wait till Christmas day, like us*)
10 True (indirectly stated: *The only pity is that they didn't legalise proper shopping before ...*)

3 1C 2E 3B 4F 5H

4 1 No (She would only like a few practical but superficial things to be standardised, such as telephones, cars and time changes.)
2 Yes
3 Yes
4 Yes
5 No (Not necessarily; it has only existed for a century.)

5 1 to wallow in 2 austerely, nothing but
3 flat, inertia 4 the only pity, proper
5 not only can't, can't even

6 **Suggested answers:**
In some ways one wishes things were more standardised.

... airline schedules are total chaos for two weeks every autumn.
But times and festivals are among the hardest things to shift.
It is the fear of losing these differences ... that makes people scared of getting close to Europe.
... my guess is that they will stay unchanged ...
What matters is not that the groupings and re-groupings happen; they always will; but whether people carve each other up in the process.
I now see it (the national resilience) as a saving grace.
... which is how it should be.

Unit 11 The living world

Section A

2 **Suggested answers:** 2, 3, 4, 6

4

Country	Wolves are legally protected Yes: ✓ No: ✗	Numbers are increasing: + declining: − stable: ----
Italy	✓	+
Finland	✗	----
Spain	✓	+
Portugal	✓	−
Greece	✓	not mentioned

5 1K 2A 3F 4C 5J 6B 7H 8G

6 He sympathises with the conservationists. In general, the writer presents the wolf in a positive light. He discusses the 'success' of the conservation programme, and what needs to be done to make sure the wolf population increases. He only briefly mentions the dangers of wild wolves; although children have been killed in Spain, he insists on the rarity of accidents. He compares killings by wolves to deaths in car accidents. However, he doesn't suggest that cars are perhaps a necessity but not wolves.

7 **Suggested answer:** a and d

Section B

1 1 He studies animal behaviour and octopus behaviour in particular.

2   He suggests that the octopus did not in fact laugh, it only appeared to '*– or so it seemed to me.*' Without the last phrase the overall meaning would be that the octopus did in fact laugh.

3   He studies animal behaviour and compares it with that of humans. He discovered echo location in bats.

4   He is likely to be critical about the analogies Griffin finds between human and animal behaviour. The anecdote of the laughing octopus is used to illustrate how easy it is to misinterpret animal behaviour by comparing it with human capacity.

2   Yes.

3   use of tools: chimpanzees, Egyptian vultures
agriculture: ants
engineering: beavers
communication: bees, chimpanzees, dolphins

4   1   It is probably a means of locating things using echoes. There are no clues to meaning in the text. The writer assumes the reader knows what he is talking about.
2   A bird. There are enough clues to guess the meaning – it flies, and has a nest and eggs.
3   It is a bird but there are no clues to meaning in the text. The writer assumes the reader knows this. It presumably cracks ostrich eggs in order to eat them.
4   She was a remarkable blind, deaf and dumb woman. There are no clues to this in the text. The writer assumes the reader shares this knowledge with him.
5   A Latin expression meaning 'an indispensable condition'. No clues are given in the text.
6   The terms are explicit and we can guess what it refers to.

5   1   Griffin   2   writer   3   writer (we don't know Griffin's opinion)   4   writer and Griffin
5   writer   6   Griffin   7   Griffin and writer

6   critical

Unit 12 Communications

Section A

2   a   We cannot believe that the writer is serious when she describes herself as important and busy.

3   1C   2E   3E   4A   5B   6B   7A   8D

4   1e   2h   3a   4g   5c   6f   7b   8d

5   1A   2A   3C   4B   5A   6A

6   The phrases are all exaggerated.
at least a day
obviously, that is out of the question
God only knows what international incidents have been averted
I am now at the centre …

Section B

2   e

3   b

4   1c   2d   3a   4e   5b

5   The use of capital letters, or 'shouting'.

6   1   True
2   False (They can use capital letters but it sounds like shouting.)
3   False (You use them to emphasise a word.)
4   True

7   Cyberspace: no clue; this is another term for the Internet
Netiquette: no obvious clue, although the whole text is about etiquette on the (Inter)net – netiquette
Beetle: no direct clue, but it refers to a type of small car made by Volkswagen
forum: special-interest group
flamed: assaulted
spamming: the Monty Python spam sketch
Monty Python spam sketch: no clue; the reference is to a sketch by a group of British comedians. Culture-specific knowledge is required to understand the meaning here.
emoticons: symbols, ways of expressing mood
TTBOMK: to the best of my knowledge
CB: Citizen's Band

Unit 13 Science fiction?

Section A

2 Science & technology

3 informational

4 & 5 Hospital robot: i, ii, vii, E, H, F
Robot technology: iii, vi, ix, B
Surgeon's robot: v, A
Domestic robot: viii, D, G, I
Climbing & service robots: iv, C

6 1H 2E 3B 4C 5A 6F 7D 8I

7 The robots refers to the two hospital robots.
A few years ago is contrasted with Now in the
following paragraph.
The latest version of the machine refers to the
climbing robot.
Meanwhile indicates a parallel development by
another company.
its refers to the keyhole surgery robot.
Other robots continues and completes the list of
robots being developed.
for example introduces an example of the
development of robot safety systems.
Its refers to Helpmate's brain.
Science fiction? refers to the development of a
domestic robot able to perform a variety of
tasks in the home.
The robot refers to the domestic robot of the
future.

Section B

2 For: 4, 5
Against: 1, 2, 3, 6

3 *mushrooms:* the Parisian mushroom has been
genetically mixed with a wild mushroom to
increase production and make it more resilient.
tomatoes: a variety of tomato has been created
which does not soften as it ripens. It can stay
longer on the supermarket shelves.
grapefruit: a variety has been developed which is
sweet, red and thin-skinned. It is expected to
sell better than its competitors.
potatoes: a variety has been developed specially
for making chips. It absorbs less fat and
therefore people who do not want to put on
weight will buy it.

4 1 … they produce more meat, milk and eggs but
which may suffer physical damage in the
process. Western farmers have already bred
cattle …
2 … it does not soften as it ripens. Supporters
say the tomato …
3 Still, traditionalists and gourmets in Europe
are fighting their development. Consumer
opposition means …
4 Questions have arisen over whether new
proteins in genetically modified foods could
cause allergies in some people. For example, if
a corn gene …
5 … the resilience of the wild strain.
'Mushrooms in the past …'

5 1 Supporters of the development of the new
variety agree with this statement but critics say
the main advantage is to keep the tomatoes in
the shops for longer.
2 Scientists behind this research believe that the
food is not unsafe, but critics say that the
consequences for human biology are
unknown.
3 Genetically engineered plants, for example,
may become virulent weeds.
4 No evidence.
5 Clearly, financial incentive lies behind the
development of these bigger, more productive
foods.
6 In the short term, much of the technology
remains untested and in the long term the
consequences for human biology are
unknown.
7 No evidence that this is likely.
8 No evidence.

6 Paragraph A: b, d, e
Paragraph B: a, c
The original final paragraph is B.
It is difficult to determine which is the original
final paragraph because the writer of the article
presents arguments for and against and only gives
her own view in the final paragraph.

Unit 14 Modern life

Section A

2 the limits of medieval man's experience
attitudes to life and death
the fight against physical ageing
future frontiers
nostalgia for the past

3 the limits of medieval man's experience: 1, 5, 6, 9
attitudes to life and death: 3, 4, 8
the fight against physical ageing: 2, 7
future frontiers: 10

4 1 *They (our ancestors) would not have known what to make of the word 'stress' unless it was used in the context of shipbuilding …*
2 No evidence – the article only states that the working day was shorter
3 *Even an eight-minute mile could not have been possible … Nowadays runners unable to qualify for the Olympics can manage this (four-minute mile) on occasions.*
4 *Even after many lessons his reflexes would have been utterly unable to cope with the new frontiers of possibility.* Also, all the examples of our ancestors' limited experience.
5 No evidence – they weren't used to seeing fast-moving objects.
6 No evidence – the text mentions unfamiliar, modern loud noises not loud noises in general.
7 No evidence – not because our senses are stimulated.
8 *… most of them (images) ill-digested, lingering in the mind only as subliminal worry-beads, recurring every now and then in the hopeless quest for interpretation.*

5 1C 2C 3B 4B 5C

6 Suggested answers:
The sirens of fire brigade and police, with their evil cadences … the sheer assault on the nerves … that stammering, stuttering abuse … not been bludgeoned into involuntary surrender by a mad montage of abstractions … most of them ill-digested … worry-beads … hopeless quest … senses are pummelled … hysterical flight before death … sad bravery … brilliant surgeons … unlikely organs … the voluntary exhaustion … orgy of hopping … pseudo-scientific name … pristine verities … stunning acceleration …

Section B

2 When you read the opening paragraph you are immediately aware of the writer's critical attitude towards psychoanalysis. So you may decide that the main purpose is to criticise. You may decide that the main purpose is to amuse the reader because the description of a typical analysis session is made to appear ridiculous. The writer would probably answer the question by explaining why he is so critical of psychoanalysis.

3 The writer is very prejudiced against psychoanalysis.
to criticise psychoanalysis

4 1 Freud's research. Approval
2 The use of psychoanalysis in modern medical treatment. Disapproval
3 the use of psychoanalysis in the treatment of depression. Disapproval
4 The use of analysis to treat people who are not ill at all. Disapproval
5 Better self-understanding through analysis. Disapproval
6 It is a waste of money. Disapproval
7 The spread of analysis as a means of treating people. Disapproval
8 Brief counselling. Approval
9 Analysis. Disapproval
10 Treatment by brief counselling. Approval

5 Yes: 1, 4, 5, 7, 8
No: 2, 3, 6

6 You may have chosen all or some of these words:
a) critical, disapproving, condemning, prejudiced, uncompromising
b) admiring, approving

7 ironic

Unit 15 Other people, other ways

Section A

2 1 smoking restrictions
2 foreign tourists or business people who smoke
3 the only remaining place where you can still smoke
4 the attitude towards smoking (in the USA)

3 The writer only presents the problem from the smokers' side. She is sympathetic to visitors to the USA and she probably thinks that there are too many restrictions on smoking.

4 c

5 1C 2F 3A 4G 5B 6D

6 1 Because they can smoke there.
2 A flaw in the American character; the extremes in American society.
3 Americans care more about everything; they hold very strong opinions.
4 They don't care about smoking and drinking habits because, unlike Americans, most people are healthy.

Section B

1 The Mohana people and their technique of using herons for fishing.
c and d

2 a)A b)I c)D d)C e)F f)B g)E h)G i)H j)J

3 & 4 1vi: *survive there* (in the harsh wasteland of the Sind plain)
2viii: *the most unusual* (of the three)
3ii: a trained heron will stand stock still above a fish (which is then trapped)
4ix: *Instead* (of breeding herons)
5i: *It* (the training of the heron)
6v: *their skills* (of heron fishing), *the lowliest of the three* (description follows)
7x: *They* (the mirbamar)
8iv: *On the other hand* (follows *On the one hand*)
9vii: *the economy* (of 20th century Pakistan)
10iii: *Yet* (in contrast with decrease in numbers)

5 1 unpleasant
2 dirty
3 held with a rope
4 quickly
5 to do well

7 The way of life of the fishermen is very unusual and is more likely to interest the general reader.
Suggested answers: regret, pessimism

Unit 16 The world of work

Section A

2 4, 2, 7, 5, 1, 8, 6, 3

3 Mr Becker is a professor at Cornell University. He studies the patterns of office work. He is trying to improve office comfort and staff communications. Thomas Allen is professor of management at the Massachusetts Institute of Technology. He seeks to improve staff communications.
Steelcase is a manufacturer of office furniture. It experiments with office layout to improve communications.

4 True: 1, 3, 4, 8, 9
False: 2, 5,6, 7, 10

5 **Suggested answers:**
1 Automation has affected office productivity far less than was expected.
2 They create a lot of wasted space and make communications between employees difficult.
3 It will become an important meeting place for workers and a company social centre.
4 The new layouts are designed to improve communications between workers by increasing the chances of them meeting one another.
5 They rarely meet their employees and their employees cannot see them.

6 1B 2B 3C 4B 5A

Section B

3 He generally approves of meetings.

4 1D: *enshrine* – to put in a shrine or a sacred place; more usually used to refer to the remains of a dead person
2G: *buttress* – to support a building
3A: *corn* – a form of grain fed to animals
4F: *round up the strays* – to gather together animals which have wandered away from the main group; often used when referring to sheep

5 1 *battle grounds:* a battle ground is a place where a battle takes place between opposing armies. In the text it refers to the meeting room where participants argue over company business.

2 *in black and white:* something that appears in these two colours. In the text it refers to written print.

3 *the shop floor:* obviously 'the floor of a shop'. In the text it means a factory production area.

4 *a security blanket:* a blanket is a cover for a bed. Here it refers to a function of meetings – they console and help managers feel better about their role.

5 *safety-net-cum-rubber-stamping function:* a safety net is the net used in a circus to catch acrobats who accidentally fall. Here it refers to the supporting and helping function of meetings. A rubber stamp prints names, dates, etc. on documents and is used to make these documents official. Here it refers to the official function of meetings and their role of representing authority.

6 1A 2C 3B 4B 5B

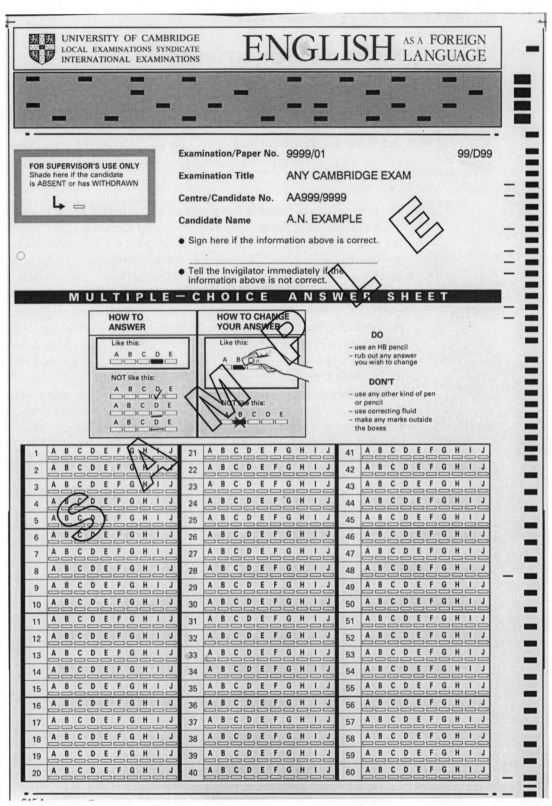

Acknowledgements

The authors and publishers are grateful to the authors, publishers and others who have given permission for the use of copyright material identified in the text. It has not been possible to identify the sources of all the material used and in such cases the publishers would welcome information from copyright holders.

The material on pp. 8 and 10 is reproduced by permission of the University of Cambridge Local Examinations Syndicate; the Canadian Red Cross Society for the extract and illustrations on pp. 13–14; Graham Portlock for the photograph on p. 16; *The Guardian* for the extract on p. 22 (by James Erlichman); Wimpy International/Publicis Ltd for the photograph on p. 24; *The Observer* for the extracts on pp. 24–5 (by Helen Lowry), p. 34 (by Sarah Lonsdale), pp. 63–4 (by Robin McKie), pp. 76–7 (by Katharine Whitehorn), pp. 82–4 (by Stuart Sutherland), pp. 88–9 (by Suzanne Moore), pp. 105–7 (by John Collee) and for the illustration on p. 105, pp. 112–13 (by Adam Baine); *The Times* for the extracts on pp. 28–9 (by David Wickers, 1992), p. 42 (by Mark Ottaway, 1993), pp 94–5 (by Nick Nuttall, 1993) © Times Newspapers Ltd; photographs on p. 32: (a) *The Observer*/John Wildgoose, (b) Photographers Library, (c) Stockfile/Sue Darlow; Voyages Jules Verne for the extract on p. 37; *The Independent* for the extracts on pp. 40–1 (by Frank Barrett), pp. 52–3 (by Amon Cohen), pp. 56–7 (by Judith Judd), pp. 66–7 (by Danny Danziger), and *The Independent on Sunday* for pp. 60–1 (by Steve Connor), p. 92 (by David Bowen); Sygma/Randy Taylor for the photograph on p. 44; *The European* for the extracts on p. 45 (by Theo Troev), pp. 72–3 (by Julie Read, Melanie Wright and Isabel Conway), p. 73 (by Jon Packer), pp. 80–1 (by Malcolm Smith), pp. 98–100 (by Keri Goldenhar), pp. 102–3 (by Peter Ustinov); Simon English for the photograph on p. 47; *The Fortean Times* for the extract on pp. 48–9 (by Paul Sieveking); *Scientific American* for the extract on pp. 63 and 65 (by Corey S. Powell); Natural Science Photos/David B. Fleetham for the photograph on p. 68; Michelle V. Agins/NYT Pictures for the photograph on p. 109; *The Economist* for the extract on pp. 116–7; Jean-Louis Barsoux for the extract on pp. 122–3.

Text artwork by Paul Collicutt: pp. 58, 79, 116; Paul Dickinson: pp. 98, 101; Amanda MacPhail: pp. 51, 78, 84, 88, 114; Bill Piggins: pp. 20, 30, 39, 120; Tess Stone: p. 36.

Thanks are due to Peter Ducker for his design assistance.